Utrecht

Sights and Secrets of
Holland's Smartest City

Utrecht

Sights and Secrets of
Holland's Smartest City

Anika Redhed

Table of Contents

Introduction   7

1. Time Travel   12
Information   23
The Rope   25

2. Tricks of the Trade   28
Information   41
To Shop or to Drop?   45

3. Bicycles and Bishops   47
Information   59
Of Flames and Fortune   61

4. Running Rats   63
Information   73
Miffy   77

5. Religion Rules   81
Information   92
The Baby Tree   95

6. Beer and Bartholomew   97
Information   108

Canals and Wharves   112

7. Practical Information   115

7.1 Eating   115
7.2 Anthem   121
7.3 Safety   123
7.4 King's Day   125
7.5 Sleeping   127
7.6 Sinterklaas   130
7.7 Transportation   132
7.8 Tours   137
7.9 Wilhelm-Ray   138
7. 10 Language   139
7.11 Peace   145
7.12 Special Days   146
7. 13 Events, festivals and the like   149
7.14 Cold Shelter   155
7.15 Going Out   156

Inspired by...   166

Introduction

"Utrecht
If you can't have fun here,
you can't have fun anywhere."

In one day you can cover over 2,000 years of history in Utrecht, the city that is home to 168 nationalities. The sights and events cater to anyone from hipster to queen. During the day you can sip a cuppa at a tea festival and a few hours later you can trance the night away at a party. Within 5 minutes you can walk from the house of the former Dutch pope to the church tower that played tributes to David Bowie and Prince. What seems impossible in today's world is possible in Utrecht; you can eat an American steak in a medieval cellar called 'Broadway' and afterwards dance a Cuban salsa in a former department store from the 19th century.

When you are in Utrecht, you should follow the beaten track: it has become beaten for a reason. And once you are on it, stray off on occasion. There is so much to discover, hidden stories and fascinating details, that a few days isn't enough to see everything. This book will help you to pick out the sights matching your interests and to see spots others don't even know about.

Once you are here, don't forget to look up. The facades in Utrecht hide so many details and stories that you would be missing out on most of the fun if you kept your head straight. Deal with the pain in your neck after you get back home. And don't be scared when a house seems to be leaning over your way. There were times when taxes had to be paid based on the amount of square meters on the ground floor. As a result, the upper floors were made bigger, so that the owners could have more space without having to pay more taxes.

I was not raised in this town, but I am a Utrechter by heart. Whenever I see the Dom Tower, rising proudly over the city skyline, I know I am home. When I ride my bicycle past the old canal, I feel ever so lucky to live here. The city is jam-packed with history of many different eras, old and modern culture, myths and intriguing shops and images. In this book I share its sights and secrets with you. At the end of every chapter the matching information has been added, including English and Dutch names, addresses and websites. Prices are not mentioned, because they are subject to frequent change. The city has not fully adjusted to foreign tourists yet, so most websites are in Dutch only. Once you get here, you will find most people speaking English and often one or two other languages as well, German and French being most common. Do ask for help when you get stuck. Most people are friendly, as long as they are not on a bicycle.

In the bodies of text, some street names have been translated to improve readability and Dutch words and street names are printed in italics. Every chapter contains a map, highlighting the main sights mentioned in that particular chapter. The numbers on the map correspond with the numbers in the text. In addition to this travel guide, there are 4 booklets covering a different aspect of Utrecht. They contain a map, sights and information in accordance with that theme. Currently available are: Water, Children, Food & Drinks, Religion. They can be purchased here: http://amzn.to/1Pu782l. Other subjects may be added in future.

The information mentioned was accurate at publication. The edition will regularly be updated when things change, however the information found in travel guides is bound to change often. We cannot be held responsible for any mishap as a result of following the information in this book. In case of doubt, contact the venue itself, or the tourist information center. We would appreciate any tips for updates or changes!

Follow us on Facebook for the latest information and giveaways: Secrets of Utrecht.

No money was received from any of the shops, restaurants, hotels, museums, etc, mentioned in this book.

1. Time Travel

There is no need to partner up with a confused professor and drive an '80s car up to 62 mph, or to hop on a rocket to break the speed of light. If you want to travel through time, just get on a plane and visit Utrecht. From cradle to grave, from Dom to DJ, you can find it all in Dom square. You can spend an entire day here. That may sound like a lot, but when you consider that you shall be traveling through 2,000 years of history, a mere 6 or 8 hours isn't much.

If you are an early bird, you may want to take it slow; nothing opens until 10 am. It is still worth arriving in time to take in the square and everything it stands for before the other tourists arrive. Find a spot in the center and turn around slowly: this is where Utrecht was born.

It was close to the year 50 when a group of Roman soldiers settled in and built a fortress. Tiberius Claudius Caesar Augustus Germanicus, known to friends as Claudius, had decided that the Roman empire should not expand towards the north. The Rhine river was to be the border and it had to be defended. Thus a group of soldiers ended up here, possibly at a spot where the river was crossable. Their tiny camp was called 'Trajectum' which became *Trecht* in Dutch. Later the 'U' was added to distinguish this hot spot from the more southern village *Trecht,* which was next to the river Meuse (or *Maas*, thus called *Maastricht*).

The settlement was quite assessable with only about 122 sqm (400 square feet), two streets and headquarters with heating underneath its mosaicked floor. You can see why interior decorating is in our blood, or at least in the veins of some of us. You can witness this yourself when you walk around the corner into Dom Street (*Domstraat*).

First you encounter 'Workshop of Wonders', interior beauty where they change the displays every few months. Should you have a credit card limit, you might want to stick to window shopping. Following this is a store filled with posters, decorative maps and paintings, among which are some modern interpretations of Utrecht. Further down there is another interior design store called *Bij den Dom*.

When you walk back towards the square, you cross a metal plate lying in the ground. This marks the place of the wall that once surrounded the fortress. You can also find these plates on the other side of the square and in Servet Street (*Servetstraat)*. At night they spread a lit haze.

By now the slow starters and tourist office employees should have had their first coffee. Pay a visit to the tourist information center for maps, books and a wide range of souvenirs. Some are good, some are of questionable authenticity. There is, for example, 'Dom Tower Tea', but there are no hidden courtyards in town where tea bushes grow lavishly, nor are the leaves fermented in local wharf cellars. I prefer the baking mold, so you can make your own Dom Tower shaped cake at home. Or the candles in the shape of the Tower. They were made by *Ruud Snel,* who was known for his candle shop. He was wheelchair bound, but still managed to climb the tower himself, on his hands and feet. Buy an entrance ticket to the Tower here, for they sell out hours or days in advance, and then head a few doors down into the art center which doubles as the entrance for 'DOMunder'.

Around the year 200 the wooden parts of the fortress walls were replaced with stones, the remains of which can still be seen. If you are lucky enough to get tickets, you are first shown a video about the history of Utrecht in which the development of the square is explained. Then you cross the old clinkers towards the stairs, which lead you underneath the pavement. This small cellar is a time travel on its own. You walk in between the remains of Roman walls and medieval church pillars to discover pottery and canon balls. At the same time, you are well aware of the 21st century. Modern sound and light effects take to you back to the devastating storm in 1674. Your torch is connected to an ear piece and, as soon as your light hits a hidden sensor, you hear the matching explanation.

This truly makes the history of Utrecht come to life.

In the center of the square you will see lines of dark stones indicating the position of former churches. After the Romans were hunted out, Germanic tribes roamed, a church was built and destroyed and built and destroyed, until, at the end of the 7th century, Willibrord came. The pope had sent him to Utrecht to convert the people in the Northern Netherlands to Christianity. Where once the Roman soldiers had slept, two churches and a monastery arose called 'Saint Salvator' and the 'Cathedral of Saint Martin'. The latter saint was popular with the Franks, who then ruled our part of the world. In the far northwest corner of the square is a gate leading to a small courtyard. A bas-relief in a wall there shows Saint Martin. In the middle of this courtyard are three stones, a modern day interpretation of the good deeds of our patron saint. Even today the holy man shows us from which direction the wind blows: on top of the Dom Tower is no cock, but a vane depicting Martin.

Utrecht became the center of the universe, although the universe was a lot smaller back then. The bishops ruled the area and more sanctuaries were built. The original church of Saint Martin was destroyed by Normans and several fires, but it was rebuilt over and over until 1254, when they decided to rebuild it in Gothic style. They started with the choir and it took a few centuries to build the entire house of God. This lengthy process was partly caused by diminishing funds. Part of the financing came from selling indulgences, but in later days this practice dwindled. The tower was built in better days. They started in 1321 and finished in 1382. It is now 112.32 meters high (368.5 feet) and the highest building in town, as well as the highest church tower in The Netherlands. Once upon a time the two lower parts were painted red and the upper part white. In 1986 a life-size painted Saturn V rocket was put next to it. Unfortunately the tower is under restoration and you can only see scaffolding until 2024.

If you have the stomach, climb up the 465 steps, enjoy the view of downtown and fall in love. If this is too much exercise for you, there are four options left: visit the city of The Hague, where a miniature park has a 4.5 meter copy (14.7 feet); fly to Japan, where a Dutch theme park has a copy that is 105 meter (344.5 feet) tall, but has an elevator; travel back in time to the year 1986, when they built a temporary elevator next to it; or take the elevator. For renovation purposes there is a temporary elevator. It should start in April 2020.

The tower has been, and is being, used in many ways. It might have served as a refuge for the bishop, a prison and a bar. During World War I, soldiers stood on top to watch out for planes. It served as a drive through for the old city tram, for the racing cyclists in the second stage of the Tour de France, and for runners of the marathon. The huge clocks are chimed 95 times a day and you can get married in one of the chapels. Every Saturday morning at 11 o' clock, there is a live concert played on the carillon.

In January 2016 the tower had 15 minutes of world fame, after the city's own carilloneur played an homage to the deceased David Bowie. A similar tribute was played for Prince in April of the same year. And then, there are legends...

In Dutch we have the expression to be 'ladder drunk' (*ladderzat*). Supposedly there was a pub on the second floor of the tower. At the end of the night, the drunks had to pass through the living quarters of the bishop on their way out and this disturbed him. To avoid this, they climbed out of the window by ladder, and often had some trouble with this, considering the alcohol level in their blood. If you didn't manage to come down properly, you were 'ladder drunk'. Truth requires that, no matter how compelling the story, there are many other legends and cities claiming to be the origin of this expression.

Another legend is partly fact. Students from one of the city's student societies (USC) do not walk underneath the Dom Tower. Once upon a time there was a suicidal student from another society who jumped off the tower, fell right onto a USC guy and survived, killing the innocent passerby. So, if you walk through the short tower tunnel, it is at your own risk.

Should you be this fearless, pay attention to the plaque on the northern side and the few small bricks above it. In 1959 a metal capsule was put in here.

This was done to celebrate the 40th anniversary of the KLM, the Royal Dutch Airlines. It contained the views of 10 well-known people about what the world would look like in 2,000. During a ceremony it was put into the tower wall by the 11-year-old grandson of the man who was then president of the KLM. On October 7th, 41 years later, this same person, now a grown up pilot, was supposed to take out the predictions. However, the capsule was stolen one night shortly before. The thieves demanded a ransom of 25,000 guilders , but it was never paid. The unknown views will forever remain a secret.

If you need to recover from the climb up, or are in need of a bathroom stop (ever since 1428 it has been forbidden to pee against the Dom Tower), I suggest you walk over to the church. Head straight towards the back and turn right twice to get to the cafe. When you walk in, you'll think you did more time and place traveling, because it will seem that you have landed in the '70s in a European country behind the iron wall, but this really is the '10s in Utrecht. Ignore the canteen-like atmosphere, as this place has one of the best views to go with your coffee. Outside lies the medieval courtyard from the city's Catholic heydays. In the gables, you can see stories about Saint Martin. In the middle of the fountain sits a reading canon. To the right stands the first builder of the Dom Tower, and in the far right corner is an intriguing detail: a stone rope. It is either an architectural joke, or the remnants of a tragedy...

Inhabitants Utrecht:	352,866
Inhabitants Holland:	17,151,228
Height Dom Tower:	112.32 meters
Number of steps:	465
Start Dom Tower:	1321
Finish Dom Tower:	1382

Make sure you feel well recovered before you continue to explore the square, because things are about to get worse. In the beginning of the 16th century, the bishops lost their power to secular king Charles V and later reformation hit town. In 1580, iconoclasm reached the church and after Catholicism was forbidden, the building was used for protestant services. In the south wall you can find a colorful altar piece. On the sides, the heads of the mourners have been brutally cut away. Also on the bishop's tomb most heads are missing.

The nave once connected the church with the tower so that the bishop could walk straight from one to the other. This was done through an air bridge, so the members of the Salvator Church (on the south side of the square) could pass to the other side of the town underneath it. You can still see the spot where the tower was connected on the side of the steeple.

Due to lack of funds, the nave wasn't built very sturdily and in 1674 a tornado blew it to pieces. The ruins remained on site for about 150 years and were used by homosexuals for secret encounters. In 1730 and 1731 several men were accused of this and sentenced to death. In the pavement on the location of the nave you can find a black stone in remembrance of this. It says:

"18th century Homosexuality Barend Blomsaet and 17 other men were sentenced and strangled in Utrecht. Their deeds concealed."

"Today homosexuality men and women choose in freedom."

Behind it stands a tall woman carrying a torch, honoring the Dutch resistance during World War II. A female figure was chosen because of the high proportion of women who took part in the resistance in Utrecht. The sculpture was revealed in May 1949 by the former Dutch Prince *Bernhard*. More statues can be found further south. The green man is Count *Jan van Nassau*. He was put here in 1883. The Count is seen as the architect of the Union of Utrecht, which in its turn is considered the beginning of The Netherlands. It was signed in the chapter hall of the Dom, now an auditorium of the university.

Behind him lies a copper ball representing one

billionth part of the sun. It has shone since 1994, when the Academy Building behind it was 100 years old and the 350-year anniversary of the faculty of astronomy was celebrated.

As you walk further, across the ground that has lived through many eras, you cross a place where German soldiers have marched, students have kissed, people have stood in the snow listening to the sound of the tower clocks, married couples have stridden in their wedding attire, students have cheered holding their freshly gained degrees, carousels have turned, where Anton Mussert founded the Dutch version of the National Socialist Movement in the '30s and brownies with worms have been sold.

Close to the entrance of the Dom courtyard is a piece of rock. This copy of a 'Jelling Stone' was a gift from Denmark for the 300th birthday of Utrecht University. It holds a story in runic about the conversion of the Danish to Christianity.

You can escape the city buzz for a bit in the Dom courtyard or in Flora's courtyard. The entrance of the latter is on the east side, close to the bus stop. Here was once a bishop's palace. After it was torn down, the open space was used for a market garden that quickly gained the title 'purveyor to the court'. This title was first given out by Louis Napoléon Bonaparte, then king of The Netherlands, a Frenchman.

It has become clear by now that a trip down Dom

Square is also a travel through different cultures and nationalities. Utrecht began with a Roman Emperor using Spanish soldiers to construct the first fortress. Willibrord came from England and had churches built with stones from Germany. Saint Martin, our patron saint, was born in Hungary. The Belgian King had his prediction put in the time capsule in the Dom Tower and so did the Russian builder of the largest passenger plane at that time. After the British Bowie died, the Polish carilloneur Malgosia Fiebig made the clocks, which were once crafted by French-born brothers, play the melody of 'This is not America...'

If you are ready to go back to the future, you can lay your feet to rest in 'Cafe Lebowski'. The interior is pretty wild and every Thursday, Friday and Saturday they have a DJ playing. If you like the past and wish to stay there, have a drink at 'Walden'. In their cellar you can see remains of the old royal palace, Lofen.

People who had fallen in love with the multicultural, multi-century square and had no idea how on earth they could ever part with it, had a solution. For 100 euros a year over a 5 year period, they could adopt 1 square meter. In return they received an official certificate and their little piece of heaven was visible in DOMunder and online. They could even add a small personal story to it. As you see, trade, in all its different forms, has also been in our veins for a long time.

Information

The Tourist Information Center

VVV Utrecht

Address: Domplein 9
Mon – Sun 10:00 – 17:00.
Web: http://www.visit-utrecht.com/

Dom Tower

Domtoren

Address: Domplein 21
Times vary. Roughly hourly during high season and 3 tours a
day during low season. Check the ticket box.
Web: http://www.domtoren.nl/en

Dom Tower Music

Automated chime music every 15 minutes. The melodies
are changed every 3-4 months. Live every Saturday 11:00
– 12:00 and from April - November also every Friday
16:00 - 17:00.
A video about Malgosia Fiebig, the city's first female carilloneur,
and her playing the chimes:
http://www.domtoren.nl/page/beiaardiers-filmpje
Tribute to Prince by carilloneur Wim Ruitenbeek:
http://bit.ly/1TJIUic

Dom Church

Domkerk

Address: Achter de Dom 1

Open:
October 1st – April 30th: Sun 12:30 – 16:00, Sat 11:00 – 15:30,
Mon – Fri 11:00 – 16:00

May 1st – September 30th: Mon – Fri 10:00 – 17:00, Sat 10:00 – 15:30, Sun 12:30 – 16:00.
Web: http://www.domkerk.nl/en/?lang=en

Dom Courtyard
Pandhof
Open: Mon - Fri 10:00 – 16:00, Sat & Sun 10:00 – 17:00.

DOMunder
Underground adventure. There is a video of it on our YouTube channel.
Address: Domplein 4
Open: Tue – Sun 11:30 – 16:30 (start of the last tour).
Web: http://www.domunder.com/en
Winner of the following awards:
Heritage in Motion Best Achievement Award, Museum and Heritage Awards for Excellence 2015, History Online Price

Bakery Bond and Smolders
Bakkerij Bond en Smolders
Cookies with honey, shaped as a Dom Tower.
Address: Lijnmarkt 9
Open: Tue – Fri 09:00 – 17:30, Sat 09:00 – 17:00.
Web: http://www.bondsmolders.nl/ (only Dutch)

A map of how the city grew:
http://www.hetutrechtsarchief.nl/educatie/199-groeikaart-van-utrecht

The Rope

*Once upon a time there was a young and dull man
called Thomas. He was madly in love with Maria
and so he asked her father if he could marry her.
He was studying to be an architect and, in order to
impress his future father-in-law, he spoke about
the tower that was to be built in Utrecht. He had
made a draft himself and wanted to enter the
design contest. The old man laughed about this
ambitious plan and said:*
*"If you manage to get the assignment, you can
come back two years after the first stone is laid and
marry my daughter."*
*He chuckled at his own wit, but Thomas was a man
in love and he headed for Holland. Since his
transport had only one horse power, he needed to
make several stops along the way. In a tavern in
Antwerp he met a man with a hipster beard gone
white who happened to be an experienced builder.
The old hipster had drawn a design for the tower
contest much better than that of Thomas, who
knew he could never compete with it. However,
Maria was at stake and the young fool did the only
possible thing a heart dizzy with love can do: he
killed the old man and stole his plans.*

*Thomas won the tender and the building of the
Dom Tower started. Every other brick brought him
closer to his wedding. In the meantime, Maria had
gone to a fortune teller and was told the marriage
would bring mischief to the both of them. Had she*

lived today, she would have lost herself in too much booze, speed and Tinder. But back then the possibilities for a young girl with a broken heart were limited and all she could do was become a nun. For lack of cell phones, she wrote a letter to tell Thomas about her decision.

For heartbroken men, the options were slightly larger and the young architect sought his relief in alcohol, thus turning into a drunk dosser. Things got out of hand and one night he ended up in the gutter from which he was saved by a priest. This made him confess his mortal sin. The priest knew that there was only one solution left for the tower builder: to withdraw into a monastery to try to come clean with God. This should give you some idea of why there were so many monasteries in the Middle Ages; everybody with a heart ache became devout.

The tower slowly rose, but the lovers' desires didn't cease. Maria couldn't take it anymore and finally took the trip to Utrecht to find her lost love. But upon arrival, she was told that the love of her life had drunk himself to death. This installed a pain in her heart that even another convent couldn't cure. She found a rope that was lying around on Dom Square and hung herself.

This happened on the first day that Thomas had decided he wanted to leave the monastery for a moment to look at the progress of the tower. He walked around, but it hurt him so much to see the construction that had ruined everything, that he withdrew into the courtyard next to the church. There he saw a shadow hanging in the corner. It was Maria.

In remembrance of her, Thomas sculptured a stone rope on this same spot. It can be seen in the courtyard next to the Dom Church to this very day.

~~~

2. Tricks of the Trade

Guilds started emerging in the second half of the 13th century, earlier than in other Dutch cities. They were very strong in Utrecht. The groups decided who could join them, what the price and quality standards were and they also limited competition by ruling that craftsmen from outside of town could only sell their goods on markets. We can still find remains of the guilds in today's town.

You can cross the Old Canal (*Oude Gracht*) by taking the Baker's Bridge (*Bakkerbrug*) ❶. It was either named after the trade or a family. There used to be a market with goods, fruit and vegetables. Nowadays it houses flower stalls. Pay attention to the street lanterns along the canal. They are placed on corbels depicting sayings, legends, stories, trades and history. On this bridge you can see one of bakers baking bread.

Next to it is the Broom's Bridge (*Bezembrug*) ❷. It was first used as a market around 1400. In later days it became an apple market and, at the end of the 19th century, the broom sellers got permission to sell here. You can see them on one of the corbels, as well as a witch flying away on a broom. You can imagine the skills the craftsmen had back then, being able to make a stick you could fly on way before the first airplane hit the skies. Although flying one was dangerous: if you were caught, you were burnt on a stake. The only way to avoid this was to get your weight measured in the town of *Oudewater*, 30 kilometers (18.6 miles) west, and get a certificate stating you were heavy enough and thus a normal human being.

The members of the guilds were also responsible for maintaining and guarding the towers around the city. These were built in the 12th century. One of the towers was called the Smith's Tower (*Smeetoren*) and it was manned by the city's blacksmiths. The pavement is marked at the spot where the tower once stood and the street leading towards it is still called Long Smith Street (*Lange Smeestraat*) ❸. There are two other street names stemming from the guilds and their tower. One is from the carpenter guild and in Dutch called the *Bijlhouwerstraat*. The other is from the tanners and called *Lange Lauwerstraat*, matching the Lauwer's Tower. Other street names refer to the trade in animals. Towards the north east you can walk down Horse Field, Pig Market and Long Cow Street (*Paardeveld, Varkensmarkt, Lange Koestraat*). The Long Feoh (*De Lange Viestraat*), where you now buy TVs and pizzas, might be named after livestock as well. Closer to the centre is the Goose Market (*Ganzenmarkt*). During the Middle Ages, this was the place to go if you needed poultry.

One of the nicest places downtown is the Fish

Market (*Vismarkt*) ❹. In older days fish was sold here and kept in baskets in the canal water to keep it fresh. Important for keeping fish was salt, hence you can now sit and have a coffee on the Salt Market (*Zoutmarkt*). Smoking was another way of keeping the fish edible, but nowadays something else is smoked on the Fishmarket. On the corner is *Cafe Andersom*, Utrecht's most famous coffee shop. They do sell drinks, but that is not what people come here for. Just walk by, inhale and you'll get the drift. Also downtown you can find the Mill Street (*Molenstraat*). For three-dimensional mills you would have to walk slightly out of the city center. The grain mill Rhine and Sun (*Rijn en Zon*) has got a new set of wings and is able to grind again. On the other side, in the Lombok quarter, you can find The Star (*De Ster*), a functioning sawmill. It was built in 1739. When the wind blew hard enough, the saws cut tree trunks into planks. They were then put on rails which ran towards the water and transported the planks away by boat. In 1911 electricity became the preference and the upper part of the mill was torn down. In 1998 this part was rebuilt to copy the original. If there is enough wind, you can see it in action on Saturday afternoons. Tours are free and possible in English. Inside is a beautiful model of a watermill.

On the southwest side of the Old Canal (*Oudegracht*) you will find several small alleys.

Though not all are equally quaint, it is still fun to crisscross through them. The Three Herring Street (*Drieharingstraat*) and the Bag Carrier Alley (*Zakkendragersteeg*) are filled with restaurants and shops. The latter is named after the bag carriers, who brought goods from the ships into town. In 1580 they got a waiting room here where they could spend their time until new assignments came in. Later they also lived in the alley. On the wall you can see a small statue of a bag carrier, which is a copy of the one hanging near Old Canal 237 where, in 1622, another group of carriers got their waiting quarters. This street also leads you towards the 'Vredenburg Square' ❺. The name refers to the 'Peace Fortress', founded in 1529 by the Habsburger King Charles V. With other countries on the lookout to invade and locals unwilling to bow to the Spanish, the building was meant to 'keep the peace'. Charles was also King of Spain, as was his successor Philip II. Up until this day, whenever we wait for the start of an international soccer game or after another Dutch ice-skater wins a gold medal, we sing that we have always honored the king of Spain. The Utrechters were, however, not very positive about the castle. It was besieged in 1576. The Spanish fired their canons on the higher buildings in the city. The Jacobi Church got seriously damaged and some cannonballs are still visible in the tower wall off the Buur Church. The Dutch didn't give up and damaged the bridges leading across the moat. This way, the occupiers got locked up in their own castle

31

and were defeated.

The city's people were afraid the fortress would be occupied again and wanted it torn down, but the officials were hesitant, afraid of Spanish opinion. The citizens decided to do it themselves. It is said that a group of women started the demolition, led by *Trijn van Leemput*. She later got her own statue on the Sand Bridge (*Zandbrug*), crossing the Old Canal holding a pick axe.

The bare area that was left after the demolition turned into a square. This was used for different kinds of happenings, from burning witches to demonstrations against left and right. Most of all it has been used to sell anything from livestock to *poffertjes*. The latter are a traditional treat resembling small pancakes and topped with powdered sugar and sometimes butter. There used to be a traditional hut on the square selling them, but it had to make way for yet another rearrangement of the square. Now there is a politician advocating a return of the hut to the city center. Hurray for politicians and the important things they do.

Markets are still held on the Vredenburg Square every Wednesday, Friday and Saturday and they have lots to show when it comes to modern-day craftsmanship. You can try the freshly baked syrup waffles (*stroopwafels*) - the smell will lure you to them - or buy some cheese, although the options may dazzle you. If you have a hard time deciding between caramelized goat cheese and the basil-garlic *Gouda*, you may want to opt for the Utrecht variant: Old Dom Tower (*Oude Domtoren*). It is made in the town of *Zeist*, 9 kilometers east (5 miles), so this is a remote connection with the city and it is even older than the more famous Old Amsterdam. For the dare devils, there are fish stalls selling soused herring, to be eaten with raw onions. Hold it up by the tail and let the other side slide right into your throat. If you do, this is completely at your own risk and we shall in no possible way be responsible for the consequences.

I am pretty sure that by now you have fallen in love with Utrecht so much that you would want to buy a house, right here and right now. Availability and prices might prevent you from actually doing so. However, you can always revert to a good old game of Monopoly, where you can buy the entire *Vredenburg* Square, as well as the *Neude* Square and Bilt Street (*Biltstraat*). Heck, you can even build houses and hotels on it. In reality you don't just need a lot of money for this, but also lots of patience. We are an organized country and one needs a permit for almost anything. So sitting down on the market and selling the soap and shampoo from your hotel room to earn back your trip is illegal. Your best bet would be to come back on King's Day on April 27th. Put on an orange hat and paint a Dutch flag on your cheek. On this day, you can sell any old crap you have in your attic; the egg warmers you knit during the times you thought handicrafts were the cure for any problem, the brown vase that even your fuddy-duddy mother thinks is outmoded, or the fermented horse milk-cucumber cookies that you thought were a good idea two years ago. Put an old piece of cloth on the ground and let out all the trading tricks you know. Relabel the egg warmers as 'vintage' and the cookies as 'organic'. Put a sticker of Utrecht on the vase and sell it to tourists passing by. If they haven't read this book, they may fall for it.

Should your attic be empty and even your kitchen drawers contain only utensils you actually *need*, bring your kid and let them play an instrument or anything else making sound. A bit of talent would be nice, mainly because you will be forced to listen to it all day, but it is by no means a requirement. Put a hat upside down in front of your offspring, treat yourself to a beer and wait for the money to come in.

This may sound a bit off to you, so maybe you shouldn't take any selfies, but for the Dutch this is common practice. There is a bit of a merchant in all of us, and a lot in some. We sell anything: food gone bad, preserved heads of Spanish fighting bulls, bewitched black cats and dentures 'as good as new'. As soon as the nomadic tribes roaming the Sahara get a proper 4G network, some Dutch guy will start selling them desert sand. You will have noticed this trait for yourself in the tourist center's souvenir section. Should you still be missing something you really need as a souvenir, like an egg cutter or a banana box, let me know. I've got a whole stack of stickers with the word UTRECHT printed in bright red letters and a hand drawn Dom Tower, that I can stick on random goods, turning basically anything into an authentic Utrecht souvenir.

On the south-east side of downtown, there is another group of small alleys ❻. The houses have been modernized but are small, with hardly any garden, and they are built close to each other. Living here is like living in a village. It has a special atmosphere. The names of the streets refer to the brewery to which the grounds once belonged. There is a Malt Street (*Moutstraat*) and a Brewer Street (*Brouwerstraat*). The Kock Street is named after the owner and the Boog Street (*Boogstraat*) carries the name of the Boog Brewery.

In the Middle Ages most people drank beer. It was cleaner than the contaminated water in the cities and it contained some nutrients. It had lower alcohol levels than nowadays. The old brewery building can still be seen by the water if you walk towards the canal through the *Lange Rozendaal*. Most breweries were close to the canals, so they could use its water and transport the beer and the ingredients by boat. Above the Old Canal behind it you can see the warehouses.

The bridge next to the old brewery building is called the Fuller's Bridge (*Vollersbrug*), named after the fullers who lived here. Fulling is a part of the cloth making process, where the cloth is cleansed.

On the other side of the bridge lies a rock in the pavement that has been attached to the adjacent house with a thick metal chain. Many centuries ago, the locals were kept awake at night because the devil and his helper played 'throw and catch' with the rock and made a lot of noise. The people decided to tie the rock down and they slept happily ever after. Further up on the Old Canal, at number 99, is *Oudaen*, one of the oldest buildings in Utrecht with its roots in the 13th century ❼. The rooms were huge and impossible to heat up in winter. For this reason, the owners built a smaller house next to it to permanently live in. If you pay attention to the facades in town, you can see this often. In later days the building served as a home for the elderly. The statues above the entrance refer to this. Its cellars now house a brewery. You can taste the results in the room that was once the hall of knights and later the dining room for the elderly. The current lord of this castle is a cat named *Dirk*. You can follow his adventures on Facebook.

There are more breweries around town, bigger and smaller ones, and their beers can be found in some shops and cafes. Brewery Maximus has its own tasting room. It is about 6 kilometers (3.7 miles) from the central train station. Once you get out there, you might as well enjoy the huge Maxima Park or the (free!) 'castle', *Hoge Woerd*. They rebuilt an old Roman fortress in a modern way, show some artifacts and pictures of the old days and they have an 1800 year old boat on display.

If beer is not enough for you, you can try something stronger: *jenever* or Dutch gin. It was first distilled in Utrecht in 1861 by Staffhorst.

The most famous shop in Utrecht is no longer a store. It is called the Shop of Sinkel (*Winkel van Sinkel*), named after the founder ❸. It was one of the first stores where they sold all kinds of different items. Today its name is still used as an expression for shops which sell a wide range of goods. The shop had a sales rhyme that many elderly people still remember. It mentions that in their store everything is for sale, from hats and corsets to liquorice and 'pills to poo'. The building is most famous for its 4 green ladies: caryatids. One of the heavy cast iron statues broke the city crane which had been standing in front of the building at the canal. There is a small sign with a picture of the crane below by the water. You can walk back up through a nicely lit tunnel, the only one remaining from the days where they were used to get the goods from the water up into the town.

After the heydays of the store, the building was turned into a bank and nowadays it is what they call a 'cultural culinary department store'. The building is as impressive from the inside as it is on the outside, so it is well worth having a drink or a bite to eat here. Check out both floors and the bathrooms upstairs, or visit for some live music, lectures, tango, salsa, French conversation, movies, fortune telling, or to knit in the company of other knitters.

There is a wide range of shops in Utrecht. On the Old Canal (*Oudegracht*) and in the Stone Street (*Steenstraat*) you can find all the brands and products that you could find anywhere in Europe. Wander a little further to find different shops, or even some very specialized ones. There are stores selling nothing but comics, board games, everything related to Warhammer, sowing machines, sheets of music, Elvis Presley paraphernalia, darts, and, of course, you can buy yourself a pair of wooden shoes.

Normally I wouldn't advise you to get a haircut when you are city-tripping, but you may want to make an exception for 'Madame de Pompadour'. Or even just stare inside through the window, but please don't leave any stains on the glass. You will see devices that look like they would electrocute you, but I assume most customers survive. I hear she also does vintage haircuts.

Now that we are on the subject of hair, a little bit further, just outside the moat, is the 'Damn Good Soap Company', which sells homemade mustache wax and beard oil. They state on their website that it is 'for beards and men'. This implies some kind of sexism, but I am pretty sure they are open to anyone with a beard. In the gray building with the circular windows on the bridge in front, they have their 'Monsieur Moustache': have a coffee while you have your moustache blow-dried into shape.

Coffee, tea and the like can be drunk in many different and often vintage places around town.

When you are looking for a spot to refuel, it pays not to judge a place by its looks on the outside. What you can see from the street is often only a quarter of what lies behind. Many buildings have a second floor, an attic, a cozy cellar, or all the above. Explore and you shall be rewarded; you never know what you may find. There is even a place on the Old Canal where you can buy an old, wooden sled together with a coffee. Or an almost antique folding chair. Or a second hand bicycle. The latter may be worth considering.

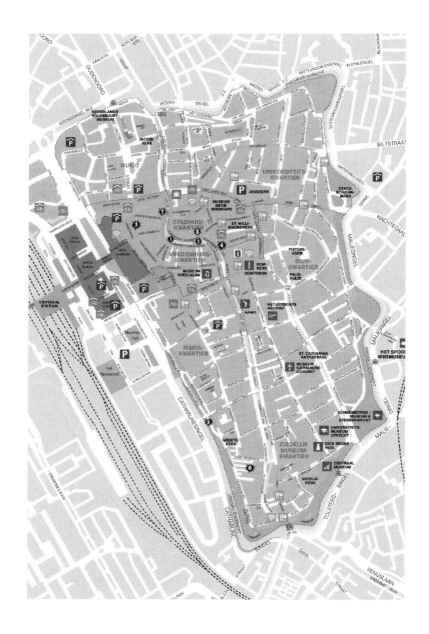

Information

Shops are closed on Sunday mornings and in the evening from 18:00 (except Thursday; 21:00). On Holidays there are special opening hours, but there are very few days where the shops don't open at all. Supermarkets are open more often than luxury shops. Check the Internet, shop windows, or ask at the tourist office.

Sawmill De Ster
Zaagmolen De Ster
Video of our visit: http://bit.ly/1WOq4xq
Address: Molenpark 3. It is a ten minute walk from the central train station.
Open: Sat 13:00 – 16:00.
Web: https://www.molendester.nu/en/

Markets:

Second Hand Market
When: Sat 08:00 – 13:00
Where: Jacobskerkhof

Textile Market
Better known as the 'rag market' (*lapjesmarkt*), selling mainly fabric and other materials for home sewing.
When: Saturday 08:00 – 13:00
Where: Breedstraat

Flower Market
When: Saturday 08:00 – 17:00
Where: Janskerkhof

Flower Market
When: Saturday 08:00 – 17:00
Where: Oudegracht, near Bakkerbrug

Farmer's Market
When: Friday 10:00 – 17:00
Where: Vredenburg

General Market
Food, clothing, books, smart phone cases.
When: Wed & Fri 10:00, Sat 08:00 – 17:00
Where: Vredenburg

Shop of Sinkel
Winkel van Sinkel
Most famous 'shop' of Utrecht.
Address: Oudegracht 158
Open: Sun at 11:00, all other days at 10:00.
Web: https://www.dewinkelvansinkel.nl/content-paginas/engelse-website.html

Noest Hout
Example of authentic souvenirs (key chains, cutting boards, Christmas decorations) made with the wood from Utrecht trees. They even tell you from which tree it was made, where it once grew and when it was planted:
Web: http://noesthout.nl/ (only Dutch)

Ouddaen
One of the oldest buildings in town and brewery at the canal.
Address: Oudegracht 99
Open: Daily at 08:00.
Web: http://www.oudaen.nl/web/en/1_home.htm

Brewery Maximus
Brouwerij Maximus
Address: Pratumplaats 2A
Open: Wed & Thu 16 – 22:30, Fri & Sat 14:00 – 23:00, Sun 13:00 – 19:00.
Web: http://www.maximusbrouwerij.nl/maximus/ (only Dutch)

Local beers can also be tasted in several cafes downtown, for example in 'Cafe Belgium' (*Kafe België*, Oudegracht 196).

Brewery 'De Leckere' gives its beers real Utrecht names, like 'bag carrier', 'Willibrord' and 'Traiectum', which has a picture of a Dom Tower on its label.

Staffhorst – *Jenever*
It is only sold in several liquor stores.
Web: http://www.staffhorst-jenever.nl/ (only Dutch)

Hairdresser vintage
Madame de Pompadour
Address: Oudegracht 268
Web: http://vintagehairstyling.nl/

Damn Good Soap Company - For beards
Web: http://www.damngoodsoap.com/en/

Monsieur Moustache - Barbershop with coffee
Address: Oosterkade 1
Open: Mon – Fri 10:00 – 18:00.
Web: http://www.monsieurmoustache.nl/

Blackbird
Coffee and vintage.
Address: Oudegracht 222
Open: Wed – Sat 10:00 -18:00.
Web: http://www.blackbirdcoffee.nl/

Elvis Corner
Address: Amsterdamsestraatweg 293
Open: Wed – Sat 10:30 – 17:00.
Web: http://www.elviscorner.com/ (English and German)

Maeson's Barbershop
Famous for being the barber for the Dutch soccer team
during the world championship in Brazil.
Address: Voorstraat 21
Open: Tue – Fri 10:00 – 20:30, Sat 09:00 – 17:30.
Web: http://www.maesons-barbershop.nl/ (only Dutch)

Barber Academy
School to learn how to be a real barber. "A professional
barber also gives advice on which beard suits best with
your face and haircut."
Address: Voorstraat 21
Web: http://www.maesons-barbershop.nl/ (only Dutch)

Werfzeep – Soap
Handmade, organic soap. Sold at different addresses.
Web: https://www.werfzeep.nl/en/stockists/

Lucas van Hapert
Artist and lover of Utrecht makes calenders, coloring
books and, yes, socks with a Dom Tower.
Web: https://www.lucasvanhapert.nl/

To Shop or to Drop?

Once upon a time there was a field named after Saint Catherine. A convent was built on it, which later stood in the way of the Peace Fortress and so had to be moved to its current location, where it is now used by the Museum of Christian Art. The name, however, still hovers around the square and our city centre mall is called 'High Catherine'. It is a good thing Saint Catherine died long before. She has appeared to people after her death, to Joan of Arc for example, but no sightings have been reported since September 24, 1973. The people of Utrecht marched through the streets in protest that day, but it was too late; the then largest overlaid mall of Europe was opened. It was the ugliest structure ever built on the west side of the iron curtain, for '50 shades of grey' may sound exotic, but when they are used in a concrete colossus they are not. When you arrive by train, you have to pass it on your way to the historic part of the city. This is why Utrecht is still under-visited. Even the people who did once have the intention to enjoy our canals and tower, ran back when they saw this 70's disgrace and took another train onwards to Den Bosch or Maastricht. So when you hop off the train, make sure to either put on your blinkers or your virtual reality glasses. After 2019 everything will be fine again. The mall will be transferred to modern beauty and the moat, in modern days filled up and turned into a road, will have returned to water. All's well that ends well.

~~~

3. Bicycles and Bishops

Many people have ruled the city in the past, starting with Claudius I. He was followed by years of bishop rule, Spanish kings and Napoleon himself. After the French, we have had Orange queens and kings and mayors were installed to take care of the ever expanding city. But today, despite a bunch of local politicians going to work in the new city hall every day, there is only one real ruler of Utrecht; the man on the bike (M/F).

The Dutch like to do things differently. Where other countries eat their cookies with a cup of tea and dust chocolate sprinkles on cake, we put them on a sandwich and call it breakfast. Or even lunch. We had an aboriginal art museum. You can walk through a medieval street, on clinkers that have been thread on for centuries, enter a stone building and dive into a world from more than 9,000 miles away. On top of that, we love to ride bikes.

In Asia bikes are being used less and less, because as soon as you have a little money, you buy a moped. If you see a person on a bicycle in northern Thailand, you can be sure it is either a tourist or a dead poor Thai. Not so here. The higher educated the person, the higher the chance they own several bikes - an old rattling one for downtown and a proper one for touring around on a sunny day. Utrecht is a bicycle city. With over 350,000 inhabitants, it is the fourth largest Dutch city, but the largest when it comes to cycling. The busiest route downtown, leading from the central train station to the university campus, counts 20,000 to 25,000 cyclists on week days. The city has built a new parking lot near the main station, the largest overlaid one in the world, for 12,500 bicycles.

We are and were trendsetters. On July 1st 1883 the Dutch Touring Club was founded on Malie Street (*Maliebaan*) to unite cyclists. It is now a general travellers' association (*ANWB*). In September 1885 the city of Utrecht designated one of the walking promenades on the same street as a cycling lane. Bikes had right of way over pedestrians and horses were not allowed on it at all. In the year 1900 there were about 100,000 bicycles in Holland. In 1920 there were 2 million.

* Utrecht: 1,000,000 bicycles
* The Netherlands: 19,000,000 bicycles
* Netherlands: 1.1 bike per person
* China: 0.4 bike per person
* Spain: 0.2 bike per person

In 2015 the 'yellow fever' hit town and everybody suffered from it. There were exhibitions showing pictures from men in shorts with bleeding knees, trees were wrapped in white cloth with red dots, the amount of Airbnb rooms exploded and so did hotel prices. Miffy turned out to have several thousand little brothers and sisters and to be an avid cyclist herself, and there were bicycles in unusual places, like the windows of restaurants and kitchen utensils shops. A bigger than life-size bike gleamed on the square in front of the city hall and a department store sold sunglasses shaped as bicycles.

For some reason, related to money, the Tour de France is now often a Tour de Europe. In 2015 the race started in Utrecht with a time trial and on the second day they rode underneath the Dom Tower and continued to the south-east of the country (*Zeeland*). The sun was shining, the city was one big party and our pride rose to the limit, seeing our beloved town on national television and beyond all day long. For one day, we were the center of the universe again. Or at least we were the center of the cycle racing world. This will happen again in August 2020 when the Vuelta, the Spanish bicycle tour, will start in the Netherlands and hit Utrecht twice.

Every year there is a 'Tour d'Utrecht' which anyone can join. You can put on your yellow jersey and sleek black shorts and pretend to be a professional racer when you ride part of the original route. The town council is considering marking the time trial the racers rode on the first day, so that every sportsman can try his best, although this could probably only be done at night, when there is little other traffic, for the roads in the city are crowded and dazzling.

That leads us to the most important question of this book: should you rent a bicycle and ride around town on a steel horse yourself? It depends on whether you are a thrill seeker or not. Should you be the kind of traveler who usually spends his vacations hanging on the side of cliffs using only two fingertips, by all means... Do you think bungee jumping is for wussies and you don't feel a thrill until you jump off a skyscraper hanging on a thread spun by your blind, rheumatic great-grandmother, go ahead.

The center is small enough to conquer on foot, but to get a real feel of Utrecht it is a good idea to wonder beyond the moats. I am a big fan of the saying 'when in Rome do as the Romans do', especially in a city founded by them. But if you choose to cycle, don't forget that the Romans were avid helmet wearers. If you follow their example you will be the only one cycling with plastic head protection. Locals can tell from the other side of the bikeway that you are a tourist and they will think you are a sissy, but at least you will be a sissy with its brains on the inside of the skull instead of having them shed all over the pavement. Even St. Martin wore a helmet when riding horseback, as you can see near Old Canal 401.

* bicycle paths Utrecht: 245 kilometers (152 miles)

According to the Copenhagenize Index, Utrecht is
ranked third when it comes to being a bicycle
friendly city. This is measured, amongst other
criteria, by facilities and infrastructure. CNN states
that 50% of all journeys in the city center are done
by bike. This could also mean that the city is a
fervent hater of cars. It is. Whatever you do, don't
take your car into town. You'd better hop on a plane
to Amsterdam or Eindhoven and take the train from
there. Or, if you must, park your car on the outskirts
and enter the town using public transportation. If
you do not take this advice, you will get lost in the
wild woods of one way streets. And when you are
driving around to find a parking space, after you
have passed the same statue three times while trying
to grow eyes in the sides and back of your head in an
attempt not to kill any pedestrians and cyclists,
wobbling over the cobblestoned streets that haven't
been adjusted to traffic since the beginning of the
horse tram era, you shall quickly come to hate
Utrecht. If you succeed and manage to park your car
for a few days, you will go bankrupt on top of it all.
And after you succeed in finding the right way out of
town, several hours after you started your vehicle,

your thoughts will be dominated by nothing else than bashing down the Dom Tower with a giant axe, dressed like a Viking. You wouldn't be the first, for there is a Norman in all of us.

As the many separate bike lanes may seem like Valhalla, they have to be shared with many others; walkers trying to cross, delivery men trying to get their goods from their trucks into the stores, pupils talking faster than they go and riding next to at least two other friends, couriers going faster than all the others and parents riding their carrier tricycles with their offspring on-board. The most charming streets downtown were built for medieval traffic. In those days the canals were filled with wooden cargo vessels instead of tour boats with glass roofs, paddle boats and canoes. Up in the streets, workers pushed carts filled with building materials for yet another church or monastery, clerks rushed by to do some shopping for the canons and occasionally the bishop rode by on his horse to see if the people were still disreputable and if there was more money to make selling indulgences.

Nowadays this job is done by the police. If the back light of your four wheeled, motorized 'bike' isn't working, or if you cross a red light, they might stop you or take your picture and send it to your home address. You can cleanse your soul by paying the fine. But since you don't enter town by car, the chances of this happening to you are small.

Should you decide to cycle through town, don't worry about the rules. They are very, very comprehensible: you always come first. Now you see the real reason why Utrecht is on the list of bikers' friendliest cities. Who wouldn't always want to come first? Some streets have even been paved red and dubbed 'bicycle street'. This means 'cars are guests' and the bicycle always comes first. I never understood this money wasting habit, for bikes *always* come first. You can stand on top of your saddle, dressed as Saint Martin, in the middle of a driving lane that has a green light and if a car hits you, it is the driver's fault.

The two-wheeled life gets better: none of the road signs were put up for you and you can even ignore the traffic lights. Roadblocks are for wimps, no matter how many fences they put up, and there is no such a thing as a 'lack of space' when passing something or someone. There is only one tiny little down side to this bicycle Buddhist nirvana: *everybody* thinks he or she comes first. Cycling through town is actually the city's number one attraction for the dare-devil tourist.

A ride through downtown is not a leisure ride. Not even in the middle of the night when the streets are likely to be empty apart from some students, but you are likely to be drunk. Why else would you be riding your bicycle through a strange town in the middle of the night? In the evening you will be competing for street space with drinking people, partying students and lost tourists like yourself. During the day competition is even worse: cars stuck in one-way land, trucks delivering coffee and vintage to the downtown area, construction workers re-cobbling or renovating the wharves, shopping women carrying too many bags, students not studying and tourists, paralyzed and bedazzled by the town's many sights. They cross roads and ignore anything even remotely related to traffic, as if they were the only people on earth. Good luck.

There are three options to obtain a bicycle. You can buy one on the street from a stranger for a few bucks, but that is illegal and not something I would advocate. You can also get one from the bottom of the canal, about 3,000 bikes end up here every year, but it might be rusty and filthy.

Your best bet is to rent one. Make sure insurance is included, because for some inhabitants of the city, stealing bikes is a favorite pastime. You will see that most bicycles have more than one lock and are attached to fences, bridges, lamp posts, or anything you can put a chain lock around. In some places downtown you are not allowed to park your bike and it might be taken away by city officials. Follow the Romans on this one.

In 2015 the city removed 17,855 bicycles, because they were either parked 'dangerously' or parked in the same spot for too long.

Make sure you know how to brake. Ride slowly and pay more attention to the traffic than the sights, if you don't want to upset the locals. It could happen though; you get cursed at. We are friendly people, but as soon as we get on a bike, the Viking in us comes out. Don't be intimidated. As soon as the other persons steps down, he or she will be friendly and point you in the right direction. Ignore any yelling. Or laugh about it, for to some of you our curse words might just sound funny.

When you are rolling, do not do as the locals do; don't ride in any direction you please. Always keep right, take the bicycle lane if there is one and never assume traffic in a one-way street only comes from one way. And of course, last but not least, don't forget to enjoy the ride and go where the wind blows you. On second thought, don't. It always blows in the direction you don't want to head.

Winds in The Netherlands are magical, for they turn at will. Prepare for wind and rain. Utrecht is dubbed by some as the 'Sunshine City', but in fact it is one of the wettest parts of our country. And if it rains, just get wet. Do not ride while holding an umbrella. That is just for pros. (Video: http://bit.ly/1OemIAZ)

It rains 6.5% of the time (officially).

Some points of interest you could paddle to on sunny days include the forest called *Rhijnauwen*, with old mansions and the remnants of a fortress. Or you can opt for the lake in the north (*Maarseveense plassen*). The 'Maxima Park' in the far west is a large and inviting municipal garden. It has art works, sports facilities, an observatory, a playground and some plane trees that once stood on the Dom Square but had to make way for DOMunder. In memory of their origin, they were placed together in the shape of a cross. The park is well combined with a visit to the newly built Roman fortress, 'Castellum', and the Maximus Brewery.

The most appropriate way to pass your time on a bike would be to follow the route past the murals in town. Some were made especially for the Tour de France. It is like a quest with some jewels for treasure. The tourist center has a free booklet with both a walking and a bicycle tour. Mind you, part of the described bicycle route leads you past the Old Canal, a section I would advise you to do on foot most parts of the day.

Should you be into modern architecture, a ride to the university campus (*Uithof*) will suit you. Do not do this during morning rush hour, for there are some students that actually do attend class.

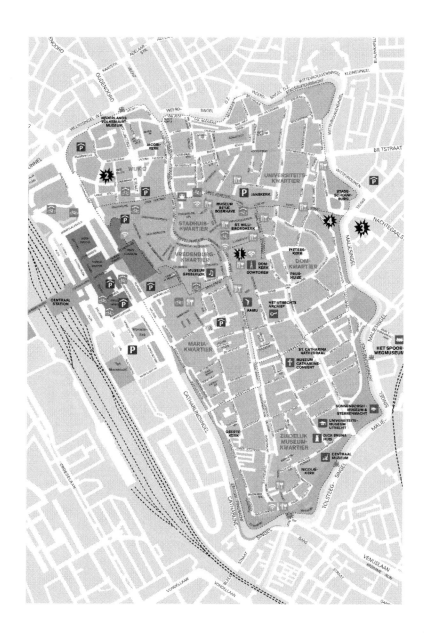

58

Information

Tour d'Utrecht
https://tourdutrecht.nl/

Parking on the outskirts
https://www.parkeren-utrecht.nl/pr

Bicycle rent:

1. Tourist Information Centre ❶
VVV
Address: Domplein 9
Open: Mon - Sun 10:00 – 17:00.
Web: https://www.visit-utrecht.com/explore-utrecht/cycling/bicycle-hire-companies

2. Willemstraat Bike ❷
Address: Willemstraat 22
Open: Mon, Tue, Fri 09:00 – 19:00, Wed 10:00 – 19:00, Thu 09:00 – 20:00, Sat 10:00 – 18:00, Sun 12:00 – 17:00.
Web: http://www.willemstraat-bike.nl/verhuur (only Dutch)

3. Laag Catharijne ❸
Address: Nagtegaalstraat 1
Open: Mon – Fri 09:00 – 18:00, Sat 09:00 – 17:00.
Address: Catharijnesingel 28
Open: Mon – Fri 09:00 – 19:30, Sat 10:00 – 18:00.
Web: http://www.laagcatharijne.nl/verhuur (only Dutch)

4. Fietspunt ❹

Moved out of the city center.

Rhijnauwen – forest

Web: http://www.fortrijnauwen.nl/ (only Dutch)

Maxima Park

Web: http://www.maximapark.nl/ (only Dutch)

Of Flames and Fortune

It has wings, a long, rat-like tail and a red beak. Its eyes are even worse; they burst real flames. One look at those and you'll burn until there is nothing left of you but a small pile of ashes.

Every self-respecting old city has had a monstrous basilisk and so did Utrecht. It was born from a cock's egg and bred by a turtle. It was the biggest monster the world had ever known. It crawled its way into a wharf cellar underneath a brewery, ready to cause trouble.

One day a worker had to go down to get some tools... and never returned. His boss went downstairs to check on him... and never returned. Many others died before they discovered there was a basilisk living in the cellar. The door was firmly locked and all wise men avoided going close. People could hear the creature's scales rattling and some even saw the red light of the flames underneath the door. From time to time, a brave, or more likely drunk, person went in, against all odds, armed with a bow and arrow or a sword, but nothing was left of them. More than a century went by with the monster playing around with the foolish. Then one day another young man wanted to open the door and go down into the monster's home. The lad was not only sober, but also young and handsome, so they tried to stop him in all possible ways, warning him of the danger. He wasn't even armed.

But the young bloke was determined. He blindfolded himself with an old rag. He fumbled his way to the door and down the stairs, keeping his eyes closed as best he could. He heard the rattling and quickly afterwards he felt the heat of a flame stroking his face. Out from underneath his cloak, he pulled a board. It had a mirror on the other side. The guy held it up in the direction of the flames. He moved closer to the danger, still unhurt.

The basilisk had looked into the mirror and the flames had bounced back from it. The monster had been set on fire by its own eyes and was reduced to ashes. The city was saved and sighed with relief. Thanks to the brave young man, you can now safely visit Utrecht.

~~~

4. Running Rats

"I am rabbit of Olland."
Louis Napoléon Bonaparte was sent here by his
famous brother. He tried to learn some Dutch and,
combined with his French accent, he
mispronounced: "I am King of Holland." In 1807 he
decided to live in Utrecht and had a few buildings
remodeled into a royal palace shortly before he
moved to Amsterdam. The premises he left behind
have been turned into a library. Walking through
the same halls as Napoleon, some old walls still
visible, you will see that they are now filled with
modern studying facilities and a grand café. You will
want to be a student again.

60% of our city's inhabitants have followed
higher education, thus making our town the
smartest in The Netherlands. The Utrecht
University is the largest in the country and,
according to the 'Academic Ranking of World
Universities', it is also the best. The buildings of the
different faculties are scattered over town, but there
was not enough room for all the students. For this
reason, some faculties were moved to the outskirts
in the '70s and '80s, creating an entire science park
that keeps growing. The area houses the University

of Applied Sciences, a teaching hospital and even the 'Central Bureau of Fungal Cultures'. Considering the era in which they started filling the pastures with stones, the buildings are gray and gloomy. Most of us who studied there are still suffering from some kind of concrete phobia. The area is improving though, with famous architects like *Koolhaas* cheering up the area. There are now some colorful and well-designed buildings too. The University Library on the *Uithof* was selected by CNN to be in the list of the world's 15 most beautiful libraries.

If you like to balance out all the brick watching, you can visit the lush and green Botanic Gardens in the *Uithof*, built around another fortress. It has a little sister downtown in the so called 'Museum Quarter'. In the middle of the buzz, hidden between regular streets and silent houses, the old Ginkgo keeps growing; herbs spread their fragrances and butterflies flutter over the pond. There are water lilies the size of a bicycle wheel (Victoria amazonica). The haven is also called 'Museum Garden', since it is now part of the adjacent University Museum. If you like to stare at ears preserved in liquid or stuffed flamingos, or if you have children somewhere between 7 and 14 years of age, put this museum on your list. The kids can put on a lab coat and pick a working station. It will have a booklet with instructions, drawers with the necessary tools and they can do their own experiments: generate bubbles in water with a battery and a pencil, or determine which tongue belongs to which animal. I wish you a lot of luck getting your offspring out there before closing time.

If you like plastic rats 'running' around on rails, you can pretty much pick any museum in town. Either they were on offer, or people from Utrecht simply love fake rodents. If you are looking for other criteria, the museum you pick depends on the age of your children. If they are between 2 and 6, the Miffy Museum will make everybody's day. You will be their favorite parent forever, or at least for the next two hours until they get tired. This is probably the only museum where kids pay more than their parents, although I am not sure if this interactive 'Miffy world' should be called a museum.

If your kids are older, take them to the lab in the University Museum, as mentioned before, or to the Railway Museum. They have beautiful and well-polished trains, most of which have an interactive display inside. There are old signs, models and an original Orient Express. And who wouldn't want to have their picture taken standing behind a flat, cupboard train guard with a hole at the place of its head? This may sound like a place for train freaks, but it is not. If you don't have any children, borrow some. Or pretend to be one yourself, because it is an amusement park in disguise. A shaking elevator will not only take you down, but also 100 years back in time to the days where the first steam engine had just been made. You can board a train and get startled because there is another locomotive about to frontally hit yours. If you survive, you can virtually ride through high, snow-capped mountains and space. At the end of the day you will be begging the museum guards to let you in the jumbo express running the grounds, or on the little boats going to and from the light house. If you are brave enough, and if you fit in, slide down the artificial rocky mountain.

If your family is large, you will be nearly broke after a day of trains. Don't worry; wander to the Archives. If there was ever a place where the name didn't match its offer, it is this one. There is plenty of digital paperwork from days gone by, as well as old books, but really this is a museum on the history of Utrecht. Some exhibits change twice a year, some are permanent. The building was once a monastery and the remains of this can be seen in the cellar, along with a talking monk. Many years later it was a court and some of the cells are being used as displays. A highlight is the carriage in which you can take a ride. It is a bit shaky, but you get to see the town and surroundings as they were centuries ago. The coachman is a bit talkative, but, since it is free at all times, there is really no reason to complain.

Napoleon's rule has left a lasting impact on our country. During those days we started using house numbers. Before that houses usually had a name, as you can still see on many facades in the old part of town. The displays on the lantern corbels often refer to the name of the house standing close to it. Under the French we got our first constitution, a registry office and family names became obligatory.

A measure with less impact was the renaming of neighborhoods, because the Dutch names were unpronounceable for the French and so they tagged the areas with a letter. The northwest of the downtown area still has this name: Neighborhood C (*wijk C*). It is known as a working-class quarter with people speaking in a strong local accent, calling the city '*Utreg*'. The most famous person who lived here was *Anton Geesink*, a Dutch judoka who won a gold Olympic medal, two world championships and 21 European Championships, but who's counting... Further north, where he used to live above his own judo school, is a street named after him. His bust was erected in the neighborhood he grew up in, next to the entrance of the Jacobi Church.

On the other side of this church is the 'Dutch Museum of back streets and popular neighborhoods'. The entrance is one of the best I have ever seen in a museum. Not an overwhelmingly huge hall with lots of white plastics and an 'I'm going to impress you with enormous nothingness' atmosphere that leaves you feeling lost, but a cosy living room. Oak chairs and tables with thick red tablecloths, the plants and the pictures on the wall all make you feel like you are at your grandparents' house. It is small, but as close as you can get to learning about the life of laborers in the past century. The video about the history of town and a booklet are in English, the other captions are in Dutch.

In the first room you can watch people talking about their lives in a local accent, if you can hear the difference. Walk through rooms with alcoves and alleys with the infamous running rat. Upstairs they show the interior of an old bakery and you can smell soap, hats and other odors from the past. Last but not least, they have a showcase with the shoes of *Anton Geesink*, size 49.5 (14.5). He is a national hero, albeit for those over 40. There has even been a march composed for him, to be played on a barrel organ. These were once quite popular in Dutch streets and you can still sometimes hear and see them with a man standing next to it, shaking the traditional coin box to collect money.

The history of automated organs can be seen at the 'Museum for Self-playing Instruments' (*Museum Speelklok*). This has to be one of the most cheerful museums in town; it is all about music. The massive organs in the dancing room play current hits as well as '60s and swing. Do wait for a tour to start, because staring at musical machines staying silent is not as much fun. The instruments don't just play a tune, but often different kinds of elements move in accordance with the tones. If you are lucky, you get to see a mechanical Van Gogh at work, or a rabbit coming from an egg, as the music box plays. More fun for humans of all ages is to be found in a free museum that is sure to cost you money. Turn off your cell phone and get ready to step back in time by about 140 years. Don't take any pictures, unless it is with an original wooden whole plate camera. Put on a vintage Victorian dress or lounge coat, although this may not fit your luggage anymore. The lighter you travel, the better. Preferably without a suitcase, because the small wheels won't match well with the old center's cobble stones.

Tick your cane through the backstreets and find the side alley within the side alley. A low door leads you into a candy store. Jars filled with sugar in all kinds of shapes and colors fill every little corner in the small room. Liquorice, peppermints, 'lick cookies', gummy bears, candy canes and many other kinds that don't even have a translation, nor will foreigners be able to pronounce their indigenous names. Ask for some typical old Dutch candy and the ladies working here will start talking and explaining. They are very passionate about their 'Grocery Store Museum'. The first floor has a room stuffed with cans, packages, molds, scales and advertisements from anywhere in the past century. Have a quick look, although maybe this is mainly of interest for the Dutch. They walk around saying: 'My grandmother had that!'

It is impossible to leave without buying anything, if it was only for the experience. The aproned ladies put your sweets in paper cone bags and weigh them on a scale using a set of weights. The total of your bill is added up on a board with a piece of chalk. Time to take out your pouch with coins, or time to get back into the future. There are likely to be some local kids spending their parents' money and there is nothing like screaming children, touching everything they are not supposed to, to bring you back in the now. That and the modern euro you have to pay with.

More history can be found at the moat. When Utrecht got its city rights in 1122, they started building the wall and, in the 16th century, four bastions were added. The first was the 'Morning Star' and afterwards came the Moon, Star and Sun Bastions. The latter is now a public astronomical observatory and museum. See what it is like to be a 16th century soldier and learn about meteorites, stars and planets. On Sundays you can stare at the sun. The Central Museum covers some of the history of the city, although the Archives do a better job at this, in my opinion. They also have changing exhibitions of modern art. Considering the prices, you may want to check what is on offer and see if it is to your liking before you go in. In the attic they permanently show the working space of *Dick Bruna,* including his bike, and also the chairs of *Rietveld* are always on display. The famous house *Rietveld,* built for Miss Schröder, is on the UNESCO World Heritage List and is part of this museum. You have to make reservations in advance and at the central location you can borrow a bike to ride to the white cubic house.

If you love to stare at bishop garments and monstrances and want to learn more about the history of Christianity in The Netherlands, you can visit the *Catharijne Museum*. There is a separate floor with some interactivity appealing to children, but the rest is a typical museum with dark rooms and lit glass displays and requires a special taste and interest in this subject. If your interest in religion doesn't go past having a day off at Christmas, you may want to skip this one. But remember, when you visit Utrecht, there is no escaping religion completely. The city was practically one big church.

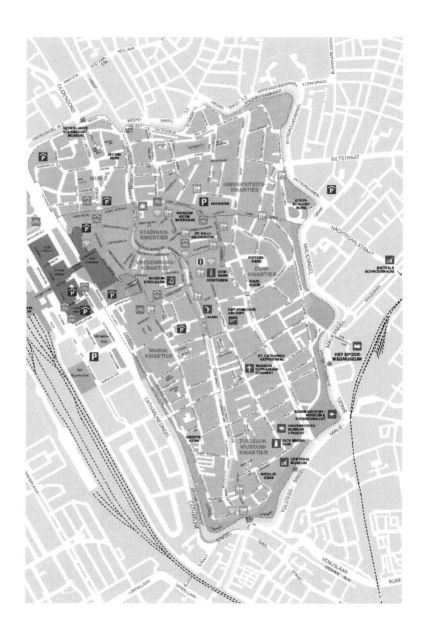

72

Information

Museums

Overview: http://bit.ly/1YbpNUj
http://www.museautrecht.nl/en/info/fancy-a-day-trip.html
(English)
http://www.museautrecht.nl/de/info/home.html (Deutsch)
All museums (but one) are closed on Mondays, except for Holidays. Never try to do anything on January 1st, April 27th and December 25th.

Botanic Gardens University Utrecht

Botanische Tuin
The large one, on the University Campus.
Address: Budapestlaan 17
Open: From March 1st – December 1st 10:00 – 16:30.
Web: http://www.uu.nl/botanischetuinen (only Dutch)

Smaller Botanic Garden downtown

Address: Lange Nieuwstraat 106
See: University Museum
Web: http://www.universiteitsmuseum.nl/english/museum-garden

University Museum

Universiteitsmuseum
Address: Lange Nieuwstraat 106
Open: Every day (also Monday!) 10:00 – 17:00.
Web: http://www.universiteitsmuseum.nl/english

Miffy Museum

Nijntje Museum
Address: Agnietenstraat 2
Open: Tue – Sun 10:00 – 17:00.
Web: http://nijntjemuseum.nl/?lang=en

73

(Because of the crowds, the museum works with time frames. Within a certain frame, a maximum number of tickets is sold. Once you are inside, you can stay as long as you like. During weekends and vacations it is best to reserve your tickets in advance.)

Railway Museum
Het Spoorwegmuseum
Address: Maliebaanstation 16
Open: Tue – Sun 10:00 – 17:00.
Web: http://www.spoorwegmuseum.nl/ (only Dutch)

Archives
Het Utrechts Archief
Used to be free! Now you pay € 2.50 over 13 years of age.
Address: Hamburgerstraat 28
Open: Tue – Fri 10:00 – 17:00, Sat & Sun 12:30 – 17:00.
Web: http://www.hetutrechtsarchief.nl/english

Dutch Museum of Back Streets and Popular Neighbourhoods
Nederlands Volksbuurtmuseum
Address: Waterstraat 27 – 29
Open: Tue – Sun 11:00 – 17:00.
Web: http://www.volksbuurtmuseum.nl/visitor-information

Museum of Self-playing Musical Instruments
Museum Speelklok
Address: Steenweg 6
Open: Tue – Sun 10:00 – 17:00.
Web: https://www.museumspeelklok.nl/lang/en/

Grocery Store Museum
Kruideniersmuseum Betje Boerhave
Address: (Hoogt 6) Temporary at Wittevrouwenstraat 30!
Open: Tue – Sat 12:30 – 16:30.
Web: http://www.kruideniersmuseum.nl/route (mainly Dutch)

Bastion and Astronomy
Sonnenborgh Museum
Address: Zonnenburg 2
Open: Tue – Fri 11:00 – 17:00, Sun 13:00 – 17:00.
Web: http://www.sonnenborgh.nl/

Central Museum
Centraal Museum
Address: Agnietenstraat 1
Open: Tues – Sun 11:00 – 17:00.
Web: http://centraalmuseum.nl/en/

Rietveld Schröder House
Rietveld Schröderhuis
Address: Prins Hendriklaan 50
Open: Tue – Sun 11:00 – 17:00.
Web: http://centraalmuseum.nl/en/visit/locations/rietveld-schroder-house/

Museum of Christianity
Museum Catharijneconvent
Address: Lange Nieuwstraat 38
Open: Tue – Fri 10:00 – 17:00, Sat & Sun 11:00 – 17:00.
Web: https://www.catharijneconvent.nl/visitor-information/
https://www.catharijneconvent.nl/besucher-information/
(Deutsch)

Miffy

*Dick Bruna, the father of Miffy, was born in 1927 in
Utrecht. He was supposed to be a publisher just like
his dad and grandfather, but he turned out to be
more interested in arts. Eventually he became a
drawer at the publisher.*

*In 1955 Dick vacationed with his family at the
seaside and told stories to his son. One day he saw
a rabbit outside the window and based a story on
the animal. His son liked those stories and Dick
decided to draw it. Miffy was born. The books have
been translated into more than 50 languages. In
The Netherlands it is mainly a children's story and
not something even 7-year olds can relate to. In
Japan and some other parts of Asia, Miffy is
popular with adults as well.*

*In Dutch, the cute doe is called Nijntje, but she is
also called Miffy, Miffi of Mifi. She has different
names in different languages:*

   French : Mouffe or Petit Lapin
   German : Nientje or Ninchen
   Finnish : Milla
   Swedish : Lilla Kanin

The museum shop in the Central Museum has a range of Miffy souvenirs. If this is not enough, you can visit either Nijmegen or Amsterdam. They have special Miffy stores selling lamps, silverware, clocks and even Miffy pirates.

In 2015 the famous rabbit turned 60 years old. This was celebrated by making several large statues in different themes. They have been sold, but some can still be seen.

The Miffy Tour in Utrecht:

<u>Street</u>: In the western outskirts of town, the modern county of Leidsche Rijn has a street named after Dick Bruna, the Dick Bruna Singel.

<u>Statues</u>: Downtown you can find the Miffy Square (Nijntje Pleintje), with a flat bronze statue of the rabbit ❶. A 3D one is on front of the Museum.

<u>Traffic light</u>: On the corner of the Lange Viestraat and Vredenburg is a traffic light that doesn't have the standard figure, but a red and green Miffy ❷.

Museum: In the attic of the Central Museum is the old workshop of Dick Bruna. You can see the books he has worked on, his desk and his scrap paper.

<u>Miffy World</u>: Across the street is the Miffy Museum. There are a few items on display, but most of all it is like a huge Miffy-world for little

kids to play in; make puzzles, plant plastic flowers in a plastic garden or climb into the lion's cage ❸.
<u>Cookies</u>: Bakery Theo Blom sells cookies with a picture of Miffy. He also sells the typical cookies from Utrecht (called sprits) and bonbons with a Dom Tower on them. Address: Zadelstraat 23 ❹.

For those that can't get enough: <u>http://www.miffy.com/</u>
For videos on Miffy: <u>http://bit.ly/1Tla2XJ</u>

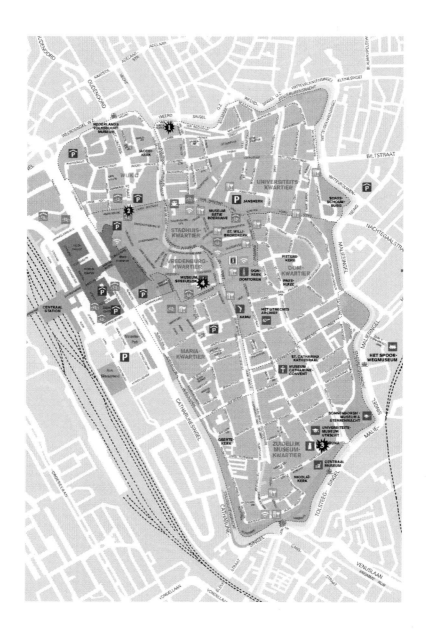

5. Religion Rules

'Thou shalt not worship trees or water.' This was common practice with the Teutons, but not something Willibrord was in favor of. He came to Utrecht to convert the Frisians to Christianity and started with building two churches on Dom Square: one for Saint Salvator and one for Saint Martin, who later became the city's patron saint. Both were for monks and canons only, not for regular people. The buildings and its inhabitants were a source of trade and employment for years to come, with fires and enemies ruining the buildings and the never-tired bishops rebuilding. The Vikings destroyed these first two churches, but they were redone in the 10th century, after which the Catholic glory days began.

Utrecht became the center of the Christian universe, or 'the cultural capital of the Middle Ages' as the Museum for Christian History calls it. Four churches were built in the wind directions. Looking at the map and the places where they were built, it seems to resemble a cross shape, but there is some debate as to whether this was intended.
Two of these churches still stand. First of all, John's Church (*Janskerk*) ❶. It has an interesting cellar with a grave. The ecumenical student community

holds its services here, as close as they can get to Willibrord, who himself is doomed to discomfort for the rest of his bronze life. Riding a horse while holding a Frisian church doesn't seem very convenient, not even when standing on a socle.

The second church that is still standing is Peter's Church ❷. Inside you can find murals stemming from the century when it was built. It belongs to the Wallonian parish and holds its services in French. Opening hours for visitors are limited to Saturday afternoons, but even when closed it is still worth a visit. There is a lovely square in front, where it feels as if you are in a remote rural village. In the street at the back of the church, called 'Behind Saint Peter' (*Achter Sint Pieter*), there are more monumental houses, as well as a doorbell in the shape of a pretzel ❸. The appertaining house was built in 1663 by a baron called Everard Meyster. Two years before he had somehow persuaded the inhabitants of the city of *Amersfoort* to tow a boulder from the moor into town. He plied them with beer and pretzels. In remembrance, he had a small boulder immured into the wall above the entrance to the carriage house, which is not there anymore. This gave the adjacent street its name. Furthermore, he had a doorbell made matching the story and also named his house 'The Pretzel'. The entrance was built askew, so that the door displaying a palm tree was better visible from the street side. Above all the owner was a poet and he wrote: 'Utrecht, she is the pearl of Europe.'

(*Uterecht, sy is de parel van Euroop.*) A wise man.
The remains of the third church in the 'cross', the
Abbey of Paul, are south of Dom Square and now
underneath a restaurant and the Archives. The
Maria Church didn't survive either, but the cloister
did and is well worth the time of your detour. Don't
forget to drink something from the green lion's
mouth at the water pump. This water was known to
be the best and some rich people from Amsterdam
had their drinking water brought over from here by
boat.

These churches were built for and used by the
monks and canons, so other churches were built for
the ordinary people. The first parish was home to
the Buur Church, the largest and richest in town.
Apart from sacred bells, it also had ordinary ones
giving notice when, for example, the city council had
made a decision or the city gates had to be closed or
opened. In later years, traffic had the habit of going
straight through the choir part of the church, so they
tore down this part of the building in 1586 and
turned the area into a street, now called Choir Street
(*Choorstraat*). In the pavement you can still see the
boundaries of the old church building.

Here you can also find a memorial stone for
Sister *Bertken*, the most famous hermit of Utrecht.
She became one in repentance for the sin of her
father, as he and her mother conceived her out of
wedlock. With the money she inherited from him,
she had a cell constructed inside the church
measuring 3.75 x 4 meters. She was always barefoot

in her unheated prison and refrained from eating meat and dairy. She filled her days with praying, meditating, writing, weaving and consulting passers-by. After 57 years she was buried in her own cell.

The church now houses the Museum for Self-playing Instruments (chapter 4). Other parishes from this era were the *Geerte* Church ❹, *Nicolai* Church ❺ and the *Jacobi* Church ❻. After the Iconoclastic Fury in 1580, a lot of the statues and interiors were destroyed. Most churches were taken over by protestants, with the matching preference for all things dull and drab. You'll notice this when you visit some of the above mentioned churches; you won't be twisting your head in awe of the elaborate decorations. For this, you stand better chances with Catholic churches built in later centuries.

Even if your idea of fun doesn't include roaming around religious objects, try to visit at least the Willibrord Church ❼. Make sure you don't miss it. It is of color and abundant beauty. There are volunteers present who are more than willing to give you a tour, or show you a few special details. Pay attention to the shelf underneath the benches; you can find them only on the men's side. They were supposed to take their hats off and put them underneath the bench. The women kept theirs on and sat on the left side, the lesser side. Above this area you can see mischievous words painted. The virtues were painted on the better, right side. Pay attention to the statue of Willibrord in the front holding a miniature Dom Church. Any reproduction of a Dom Tower is of interest to a Utrechter by heart, but this one is in particular: Willibrord died in 739 and the tower was built in the 14th century. But then, in religion miracles are never far away. Some of his bones rest in a chest in the church's baptismal chapel.

If this hasn't yet converted you, or should you have succumbed to the practice of worshiping trees or water, you can clean your soul at the Augustine Church ❽. You can confess in Dutch and English and, on Tuesday and Thursday, even in French, Italian and German. The church has a worthy exterior with its four pillars beside the canal. It is all white inside, but quite impressive with several statues.

Our religious influence in medieval times extended as far as Rome. In January 1522 a man by the name of *Adriaan Floriszoon Boeyens* was elected pope, after 11 rounds of voting. This prince of the church, better known as Adrianus VI, was born in Utrecht as the son of a carpenter and the only pope there has ever been from the Dutch lowlands. He was in Spain at the time and had to go to Italy by boat, crossing the Mediterranean Sea which was filled with Turkish pirates. He didn't arrive until August. He went into town on the back of a donkey and decided to live in Rome, although he was advised not to because of the raging plaque. He said it was to comfort the people during their hardship and to restore order. He was very strict and preferred a barren life. No more opulent dinners, gold digging cardinals, or weapons. The priests even had to shave their beards. Had he been on Facebook, his page would have been filled with spammers calling him 'barbarian from the North' and 'videbimus', the latter being Latin for 'we shall see' because of his indecisiveness. He didn't have a lot of fun in the Italian capital and died a little over a year later, in September 1523.

The Italians did not choose a foreign pope for the next 455 years. Rumor has it he might have been poisoned, but for those days he was quite old at 64. He had hoped to retire in Utrecht one day and in 1517 he had a house built for himself. Adrianus never even saw it, but the building is still called 'Pope House' and since 2015 there has been a modest statue of him in front of it. The facade is done in 'bacon' style, with layers of red brick alternating with natural stone. It has a stepped gable and a facade statue depicting 'Salvator Mundi', because Adrianus was also canon of the Salvator Church on Dom Square. He was raised in a house on the Old Canal (*Oudegracht*), which was later turned into a girls' school. There is a commemorative plaque on it.

The Pope House was sold into private hands and has since been used as a restaurant and a hotel. The wife of King Louis Napoleon spent one night in it with her son and sometime later, Napoleon himself used it as a residence for a few months until the palace he was building in Utrecht was finished. Pope John Paul II visited it in 1985 and one of our many princes had his wedding ceremony here. It is now the official residence of the King's Commissioner and serves a ceremonial function. Also it is used for parties and meetings. There are four beautiful rooms on the ground floor which can be seen in a free tour every last Sunday of the month ❶ ❶.

There is no escaping the religious roots of the city. Not even if you attend a football game. Few things seem more removed from church than a stadium filled with soccer fans, especially if you could hear what some of the hooligans shout. But these same fanatics wear scarves in the colors of our local FC Utrecht. Just because in the 4th century some guy named Martin decided to go out, there are now T-shirts, alarm clocks and even soothers in red and white. On some days, even the Augustine nuns sit on the stand, wearing matching scarfs.

It was a sunny day. Or a cloudy day, but a day it was for sure. A young man rode his horse through the fields, stepping or trotting, nobody knows. Maybe he was worrying about the people around him worshipping pine trees, or about the girl he had met the night before in the tavern 'The Gaping Goose'- we will never know for sure. But on he went. Close to the gate of the city of Amiens in

87

the North of France, he saw a beggar dressed in rags. Being a soldier in the Roman army, half of Martin's clothes belonged to the Roman Emperor and he couldn't give them away. But the other half were his to give, so he took out his sword and cut his cloak into two pieces, giving one part to the poor man. Martin himself was now only half covered in his red coat, thus showing his white undergarment.

Later in his life, Martin became an exorcist, a hermit and a bishop, performing a few wonders along the way, like bringing a diseased child back to life and curing a leper. He made himself quite popular this way and so Willibrord named one of the Dom Square churches after him. He became the patron saint of Utrecht and a bunch of other towns in both The Netherlands and Europe.

You can see the life of Martin depicted in stone inside the courtyard of the Dom Church. He is on top of the Tower, rides a horse on the Old Canal, is depicted in a wall hanging in the grand wedding room of the town hall and can be seen at many more locations in town. Most of the time he is shown on a horse with a cloak and a sword.

Despite his wonders, I doubt if Martin could have foreseen that the wristwatch would be invented many years later and be sold in the colors of his clothes in remembrance of him. Our coat of arms is a diagonal red and white and can be found in many places, including the street lanterns. Martin was on the coat of arms as well, but was removed when

Charles V became the ruler instead of yet another bishop. In 1948 Martin was put back and in 1994 removed for the second time. Despite all this, we will never forget him. Whenever we get married, or whenever FC Utrecht scores a goal, we think back to his underwear.

November 11th is the day we celebrate Saint Martin. In the Middle Ages it was a big feast. People went out to drink and eat, lit bonfires and the poorer ones walked by the houses of the rich, holding torches, hoping to get something. Nowadays children walk past the doors with lanterns, they sing a song and get some candy. In the old days, people often ate geese, for it was these animals who gave Martin away: when he was chosen to be bishop, he didn't feel up to the task. He fled and hid in a goose pen, but they started quacking and gave his hideout away. Luckily people decided to blame it on the geese, instead of on the person who was silly enough to hide amongst a bunch of birds and think they wouldn't make any noise.

So when people bought their poultry on the Geese Market, they would have seen the Dom Tower being lit with candles. The church bells rang and there were markets, musicians and charlatans out in the streets. After the Reformation the celebrations were not allowed anymore, but there has been a revival. The weekend before November 11th there is a special market in the downtown area. All kinds of art are on offer that you can't find on a normal market. There is street theater and music, exhibitions on the theme, a mass and there are several initiatives encouraging us to help the poor or lonely people in town. The highlight is the parade on the Saturday night before, with home-made light sculptures shaped as tea pots, apples and even dresses. But the first sculpture in the row is a life-size, lit display of Martin on a horse, wearing a red coat.

There were many festive events in the so-called Dark Ages. They often had some kind of religious origin and so many vanished after the protestants took over, but we are recovering. In a weird kind of 'revenge of the Catholics' there is now a cafe in an old clandestine church and it is one of the nicest settings in town to have a beer or meat loaf ❶ ❷. And there is more: Utrecht is a city that does sleep, but when we are awake, we ride our bikes from fair to festival.

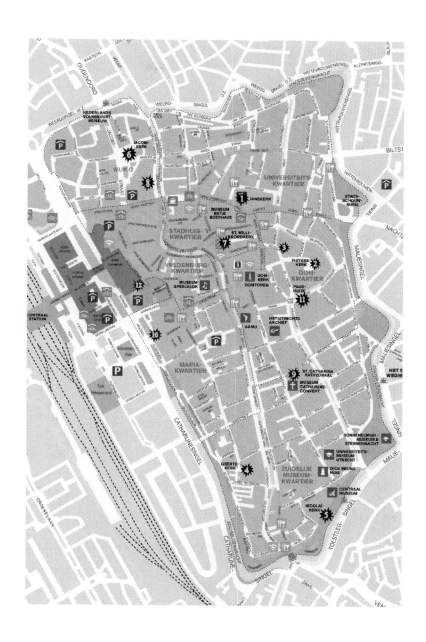

Information

Religious sights:
Video with an overview: http://bit.ly/1XbNxZ7

John's Church ❶
Janskerk
Address: Janskerkhof 26
Web: http://www.janskerk-utrecht.nl/ (only Dutch)

Saint Peter's Church ❷
Pieterskerk
Address: Pieterskerkhof 5
Web: http://pieterskerk-utrecht.nl/ (only Dutch and some French)

Pretzel House ❸
De Krakeling
Address: Achter Sint Pieter 50

Saint Gertrude's Church ❹
Geertekerk
Address: Geertekerkhof 23
Web: https://utrecht.remonstranten.nl/ (only Dutch)

Saint Nicholas' Church ❺
Nicolaikerk
Video of the chimes: http://bit.ly/1U8FF7p

Address: Nicolaaskerkhof 8
Web: http://www.nicolaikerk.nl/ (only Dutch)

Saint James' Church ❻
Jacobikerk
Address: St. Jacobsstraat 171
Web: http://jacobikerk.nl/ (only Dutch)

Saint Willibrord's Church ❼
Willibrordkerk
Address: Minrebroederstraat 21
Open: Tue – Sat 13:00 – 17:00.
Web: https://sintwillibrordkerk.nl/ (only Dutch)

Saint Augustine's Church ❽
Augustinuskerk
Address: Oudegracht 69 CLOSED for restoration
Web:
https://www.katholiekutrecht.nl/geloofsgemeenschappen/augustinus/ (only Dutch)

Utrecht has two official Cathedrals:

St. Catherine's Cathedral ❾
Sint-Catharinakathedraal
Address: Lange Nieuwstraat 36
Web:
https://www.katholiekutrecht.nl/geloofsgemeenschappen/catharina/ (only Dutch)

St. Gertrude's Cathedral ❶❶
Sint Getrudiskathedraal
Address: Willemsplantsoen 2
Web: http://utrecht.okkn.nl/ (only Dutch)

93

Pope House ❶❶

Paushuize

The house can be visited every last Sunday of the month. It is free. Show up at 11:00.

Address: Kromme Nieuwegracht 49

Web: http://www.huizemolenaar.nl/portal/en/paushuize-en/

Cafe in clandestine Church ❶❷

Biercafe Olivier

Address: Achter Clarenburg 6A

Open: Mon & Sun 11:00 – 24:00, Tue, Wed 10:00 – 24:00, Thu – Sat 10:00 – 02:00.

Web: http://utrecht.cafe-olivier.be/ (only Dutch)

A special guide about Utrecht and religion can be found here: http://amzn.to/1Pu782l

The Baby Tree

Despite our city being the smartest, and having a grand science park in our outskirts, some occurrences will forever remain unexplained.

A long time ago there was a carpenter who had gone out for a drink after work and had one too many mugs of wine. One thing led to another and he became a little bit too dizzy. After his colleagues left, he sat alone when a child came in, filthy and bold, and begged for money. Arnold, the carpenter, gave him something to eat and drink and then left. He noticed the clock on the tower had gotten five hands all of a sudden and then he walked in the wrong direction. He was somehow aware of this, but still kept going as he felt a hand pushing him even further. It was an old pilgrim who told him he was going in the right direction:

"I overheard you in the tavern. You said you are without child, but you are a good man. Keep going and within a year you shall be playing with your firstborn."

Arnold knew for sure now that he was drunk. When he looked around he saw nobody anymore, but still kept walking towards the convent. Next to it he heard some voices saying:

"Pick me, pick me, I shall be good."

He looked up and he saw several babies dangling from a tree, warmly wrapped in cloth. He actually climbed up and picked one. While holding the child, he was back at his house within seconds. As he saw his wife, he noticed that the baby had turned into an apple. She ate it and within a year gave birth to their first offspring.

I haven't heard of any similar stories ever since, but still, you may want to be careful eating apples when you are here. Though you may experience another small miracle yourself when you roam the old streets of our town. Your chances are better at this, of course, if you believe in them. Or if you stand in front of a coffee shop too long, inhaling the sweet smell of pot.

~~~

6. Beer and Bartholomew

Have you always wanted to walk through an
inflatable brain, or find your way through a maze
made out of cardboard boxes? Visit the city on a
'Cultural Sunday'. Six times a year Utrecht is one big
playground, following different themes like 'science'
or 'battle'. On these days the downtown area is filled
with people and activities. There is live music, plays
and comedy in theaters and bars, exhibitions,
lectures, workshops, quizzes, tours and most of it is
free. There is so much on offer, something will
match your taste. Plan your visit wisely and enjoy
the complementary culture, brought to you by the
Celebration City.

There is plenty of night life with cafes and dance
parties and there seems to be a festival of some kind
going on every other weekend. This ranges from
beer to animated movies, from tea to old music. In
the 'Year Fair', a 100,000 square meter convention
center, there is always something going on. There
are comic conventions, a winter circus, musicals and
fairs about walking, biking, food, records and
vacations, among many others. The list is huge.
  There isn't much you cannot do in Utrecht: play

boules in a bar, capoeira, gay squash, Lacrosse, Quidditch, Floorball, axe throwing and tejo (a Columbian, explosive version of boules) there are more possibilities than you can imagine. Every Friday night in the better season there is a skate parade. Put on your in-liners and enjoy the city in a non-touristy way. Every Thursday night in the warmer months there is free tango dancing on the square behind the city hall.

It sometimes makes me wonder why I still travel. When you live in Utrecht, you have got the whole world in your home town. There is the Committee against Bullfighting, a Tolkien Society, a mahjong club, stamp society and 'awesome space', the place to play Pac Man and other retro games the old-fashioned way. There is a men's support group, a didgeridoo school, a Carnival Federation and a Guatemala Committee. There are 168 different nationalities living in the city and you can eat from all over the world, including Ethiopian, Indonesian and Argentinian food. You can see why Utrecht is a 'divercity'. The only thing we lack is a mountain, but this is partly made up for by the Snow Sport Center Utrecht, the largest indoor ski- and snowboard school in the world. You can even skydive - not from the Dom Tower, but indoors. Nothing is impossible. Despite our 'sun-shine'-nickname, you can ice-skate on an ice rink in an outlying district year round. Pre-Christmas there is a small track on the Neude Square.

Skating on frozen water is one of our national

sports, the other is football. Not surprisingly, the Dom City rocks in this respect as well. Our country's biggest feat was winning the European Cup in 1988 and four of the winning team were from Utrecht. Our city's football club plays in the country's highest division. Outside the national three top clubs (Ajax, PSV and Feyenoord), it is the only team that has never been relegated from this top league and also the first outsider to win the Dutch cup. They play in a stadium called *Galgenwaard*. This name refers to the Middle Aged 'gallows field'. Don't worry, it is safe to go and watch a match. The fans have only once torn down the stadium, in 1981, when it had to be demolished to be replaced by a newer version.

Even our local IKEA recognizes the importance of sports. On the south side of town is a 'furniture boulevard', including the Swedish giant. And since the people of Utrecht apparently have an ongoing need for tables and book cases, they wanted to expand. The only thing in the way was a football field, but this was solved in the most elegant way: the pitch is now on top of the parking garage.

More quiet entertainment can be found in some of the games stores. There are a few that specialize in the less common board games. In The Joker you can always join on Saturday night to play games with locals. Most games are in English anyway. The players decide what is played, so you could end up racing your plastic horse in a Roman arena or stealing paper treasures from a Dutch guy you have never met before.

During the day street fishing is an option. It is becoming more and more popular, although you don't see people standing along the canals holding a rod on a daily basis yet. Don't think of it as an additional meal, for the motto is 'catch, photo & release'. You would have to buy a permit though.

Another tranquil 'sport' is to find the city's courtyards and alms houses. Between the 13th and 19th century it was not unusual for rich people to build small, one-room houses for the poor and needy. Some people thought this would give them a better chance of going to heaven. Some of the oldest buildings downtown were once built as so called alms houses, in Dutch also referred to as 'God's chambers' because they were built for God's will. As well as free living, the inhabitants often also received food, fuel and money. Most of these houses can be found in the Museum Quarter. An example is a row of crooked little buildings in the Agnieten Street (*Agnietenstraat*), close to the Miffy Museum. These small apartments were built in 1651 by a lady called *Maria van Pallaes*. Her family crest is depicted above every door. On the corner of Agnieten Street and the New Canal (*Nieuwegracht*) is the main building which served as the refectory; a common dining room. Above its door you can read in old Dutch that Maria was driven by God's love as she built these chambers, not wanting the goodwill of anything earthly, but a place in heaven. When you are done reading, take note of the doorbells in a beautiful clash between old and new.

Once you are finished here, quickly cross the street to the park to stroke the bronze Biru, a chow chow that was once the pet of local sculptor Joop Hekman, who lived in the old chambers and whose dog often slept on the bridge.

Another example of a row of houses for the poor can be found in one of the small alleys going west from the Old Canal, the Bag Carrier Alley (*Zakkendragerssteeg*). They are official national heritage buildings and the old facades form the front of a restaurant. Another row of alms houses along the moat have a common backyard which is now a small courtyard with a statue of one of Utrecht's writers. The main building of these 'Brunt's chambers' (*Bruntskameren*) has an eye-catching, baroque gate. Following a will from 1742, they still hand out money to the elderly here every quarter.

Not everybody was this concerned with the needy though. Some richer people built their houses on the other side of the water and an artificial mound was raised so that they wouldn't have to look at the poor from their windows.

In later days the alms houses were not built in rows, but in a square around a yard. A nice example can be found a short distance outside the city centre, with the impossible name *Speyart van Woerden*. It can be combined nicely with the bicycle tour past the murals. On the other side of town is the 'Star

Court Yard' (*Sterrehof*), where the houses have been turned into expensive freehold flats. It is enclosed between the regional courthouse and a remarkable brick building which belongs to the Dutch Railway Company and is dubbed 'ink pot'.

A salient detail in most of the histories of these alms houses is that they were saved by squatters. Most places deteriorated and did not meet modern standards and were therefore on the list to be demolished. Because of protests and their occupation by squatters, the houses have been renovated and are now official monuments.

Churches also offered living space for the elderly and built similar courtyards. One of the most enchanting and possibly unknown parts of town is the Maria Corner (*Mariahoek*). It is a mix of monuments from different centuries, including some almoner houses. More peace and quiet can be found on the northern side of Doelen Street (*Doelenstraat*) in a garden that once belonged to the Saint Nicolas Monastery. Less picturesque is the Andreas Courtyard.

Lush is the city garden right behind the Old Canal (*Oudegracht*), which doesn't have a name. The best entrance is from Spring Street (*Springstraat*) through the blue gate of a former orphanage. The garden belonged to a monastery (*Regulierenklooster*) and was later turned into a 'guest-house', a place where the ill and the elderly were taken care of. These houses arose after the Middle Ages and form another source of the city's old buildings. They were often founded by churches. The large halls were filled with beds often facing the chapel or a pulpit. In later centuries they were also run by the civil society. The Catherine's Guest House, belonging to Saint Catherine's monastery (housing the Museum of Christian History), was later turned into an Academic Hospital. This is now the University Medical Center.

The Bartholomew Guest House started in 1367 as a place where visitors from outside of town could spend the night and have something to eat. This didn't last long and some years later it was turned into a house for the ill, with separate halls for men and women. It is now a nursing home with an, obviously, long history. The members of the supervisory board are still called 'regents' and have the most beautiful meeting room in town. There are guided tours every Sunday morning at a small price, money that is used to benefit the home. The guides speak several languages.

Up until the publication of this book, this last tip was still a well-kept secret and it is definitely off the beaten track. Should this still be too touristy for you, here are some alternatives.

Why not try your hand at a game of Farmer's Golf? You walk through a pasture and you have to hit a leather ball into the dug holes. You do this with a special stick: a club with a wooden shoe at the end. How Dutch can you get? There is a 'track' close to Utrecht in the town of Bunnik, so you could combine it with a visit to the *Rhijnauwen* forest.

Feel the wind blow through your hair, smell the scent of original Dutch cow manure and remember you are - sort of - following the footsteps of 17th century students.

Back in those days there had been complaints of the city being boring, so in 1637 a permit was given to locate a track to play the 'mallet game' (*maliespel*). It was played with a stick that had a kind of mallet ending, a ball and goals - poles that the ball had to be hit towards. In the middle of the track a gate had to be passed. The poles at the end had the city's coat of arms and two duplicates have been placed in remembrance. Word has it that even the French king, Louis XIV, was enchanted by our track, which was paved with sea shells and had wooden side panels marked with the distance. A real beauty in its days. As the students played, more and more people came to watch and tea houses and other caterers popped up. It became the town's hotspot.

Hypes came and went, even in the days when they weren't called 'hypes' yet. More than a century later the game was dead. The wide street was used by Napoleon Bonaparte to show off his arms, for the first bicycle path of the country and for horse races. Even the Nazis recognized the street's beauty. The headquarters of the Dutch Socialist Movement were situated here, as were the local divisions of Hitler's Defence Force, Security Service and the German Air Force. Oddly enough, even the Resistance was present here. Therefore, a book about Utrecht during World War II is called 'At the Malie Lane'.

It is still a wide, tree-lined street with a dignified allure. In the '80s a statue route was started that now has 17 sculptures. Everybody knows the name of this street, but few know what the Malie Lane (*Maliebaan*) was originally built for. So when you meet a local, you can be the clever clog.

The Dutch like to be entertained and, since they seem to have plenty of money, they like to follow workshops that serve no other purpose than to keep them busy. In a beautiful location in a wharf cellar you can join them and cook or paint. Since you travel to experience new things, you may want to opt for an afternoon of slipper pimping. I can't think of any single reason why a sane person would voluntarily do so. Buying new ones would be cheaper, but who cares? You are traveling, so you have an excuse: you want to meet locals and do stuff you would never do at home.

For the real adventurous traveler: pimp a clog. I don't know anyone who ever did, and if I did, I wouldn't admit to it. But as a tourist you get away with this. They give you a plain wooden clog and off you go; paint, glue pieces of lace on it and sprinkle glitter. You can take the clog home and hang it next to your front door. It will show everyone you are a world traveler who knows no fear. If asked about it, just shrug as if you do these kind of activities all the time. Mumble something like, 'been doing some things with the locals, ya'know, I don't do tourist stuff'. Just make sure you don't brag about it when you are still in Utrecht. Stick to the Malie Game for this as long as you are still here. Or, instead of showing off your knowledge, you can share some tall tales.

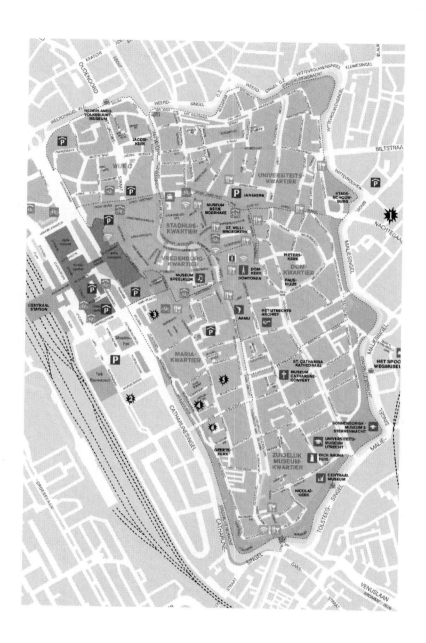

107

Information

Cultural Sunday
Culturele Zondag
Where: Everywhere downtown, start at the city hall bridge.
Web: http://www.culturelezondagen.nl/english

Dance Parties
Web: http://partyflock.nl/city/2:Utrecht (only Dutch)

Festival Schedule
Web:
http://www.uitagendautrecht.nl/genre/festivals#container
(only Dutch)

Cultural Programme of Utrecht (theater, music,
museums, dance, and so on)
Web: http://www.uitagendautrecht.nl/ (only Dutch)

Programme **Year Fair**
Jaarbeurs
Web: http://www.jaarbeurs.nl/en (English)

Skate Parade
About 25 kilometers / 15.5 miles
Where: Starting point at Lucasbolwerk
When: Fridays 20:00 – 22:15. Beginning of May until the end of
September.
Web: http://u-skateparade.nl/ (only Dutch)

Tango outside by 'Las Nueve'
Where: Square behind city hall, Korte Minrebroederstraat
When: Every Thursday 20:30 – 23:00 in the warmer months.
Web: http://www.lasnueve.nl/ (only Dutch)

Retro Computer games at 'Awesome space'
Where: Marco Pololaan 8-10
When: Every Wed & Fri night 19:00 – 23:00.
Web: https://awesomespace.nl/

Indoor ski- and snowboard
Snow Sport Center Utrecht
Address: Otto Hahnweg 23
Open: Mon, Wed, Thu, Fri 09:00 – 23:00, Tue 14:00 – 23:00,
Sat & Sun 09:00 – 20:00 in winter (September – March). In
summer only lessons.
Web: http://www.snowsportcenter.nl/ (only Dutch)

Indoor Skydive Center Utrecht
Address: De heldinnenlaan 1
Open: Mon – Wed 13:00 – 19:30, Thur 12:00 – 19:30, Fri 10:00
– 19:30, Sat 10:00 – 18:30, Sun 10:00 – 17:30.
Web: https://cityskydive.nl/en/home/3

Indoor ice-skating
Vechtse Banen
Address: Mississippidreef 151
Open: Different times in winter and summer. Check the
website.
Web: (only Dutch) https://vechtsebanen.nl/#

Games Store
The Joker
Address: Oudegracht 230A
Open: Mon, Tue, Wed 10:00 – 18:00, Thu, Fri, Sat 10:00 – the
end of the game.
Web: http://www.the-joker.nl/ (only Dutch)

Street Fishing
You need a permit. For one week this will cost €5 (2020).
You have to apply for one at least 2 weeks in advance via

this address: info@auhv.nl

Courtyards:

Speyart van Woerden ❶
Address: Kerkstraat 41-73

Star Court Yard ❷
Sterrehof
Address: Sterrenbos 83

Maria's Corner ❸
Mariahoek
Where: South side of the street called Mariastraat.

Andreas Courtyard ❹
Andreashof
Where: Between the streets Geertebolwerk and Andreasstraat

City garden without a name ❺
Where: In between the four streets Springweg, Oudegracht,
Zwaansteeg and Brandstraat.

Bartholomew Guest House ❻
Bartholomeus Gasthuis
Address: Lange Smeestraat 40
Web:
http://www.bartholomeusgasthuis.nl/Huis_in_de_Wijk/tento
onstelling.php (only Dutch)
Send an email to: teamwelzijn@bartholomeusgasthuis.nl to
make a reservation for the Sunday morning tour. Let them
know in advance which language(s) you speak.

Farmer's Golf

Boerengolf

Organized by Restaurant 'Vroeg'. You have to be with a party of at least 2.

Address: Achterdijk 1, Bunnik

Web: http://www.vroeg.nl/arrangementen/groepen-2/ (only Dutch)

Indoor Golf

Home Course

Real clubs (your own), real balls, almost 60 virtual courses.

Address: St. Laurensdreef 28

Web: https://homecourse.nl/ (Dutch only)

Workshops

E.g. *Grachtenatelier*

Address: Oudegracht 185 Wharf Side

Web: http://www.grachtenatelier.nl/ (only Dutch)

If you are not a group, you have to go to one of the so called walk ins (*inloop*). Reserving in advance is advisable. Walk ins: https://www.grachtenatelier.nl/inloop-workshops/ (only Dutch) Or google 'workshops Utrecht'.

The Team Building

Axe throwing, tejo, lava floor, workshops, escape rooms.

Address: Admiraal Helfrichlaan 6 (outside city center)

Web: https://www.theteambuilding.nl/

Canals and Wharves

Once upon a time there was a river (Vecht) meandering its way through the land, undisturbed by human hands. But sooner or later, humankind mingles with everything.

The northern part of the Old Canal was already dug in the 10ᵗʰ century. The rest of it was dug in the 12ᵗʰ. A dam was built in the Rhine and that reduced the water levels, making the chance of floods smaller, but also reducing the water levels and making it harder to cross by boat. The canal enabled transportation through the busy trade town. The sand that was dug up was used to heighten the banks on which houses were built and roads were formed. With the water level becoming more consistent because of the dam, the wharves slowly gained their shape.

The houses had storage cellars underneath. The goods from the boats were brought up to the roads and they were taken down again into the houses until somebody had the idea to dig a tunnel from the wharf into the cellar. The merchandise could now be moved straight from the boat into the storage rooms. The tunnels were later enlarged to serve as storage space as well. Some were even extended underneath an adjacent street or bridge. This waterway had been called New Canal, until the end of the 14ᵗʰ century. A new canal was dug as a drainage channel and this water was now called the New Canal, giving the other one its current name: Old Canal.

The waterside was very busy. There was always a lot of trade going on in the town and most transportation took place by boat. Some cellars were rented as homes and the wharves were used for gardens, sheds, storage and chicken cages. Most lots were fenced off, but they had to leave a small space free near the waterside. This was used as a towpath for the vessels.

The water was used by the breweries and tanneries and to extinguish fires. Every household was required by law to keep one or several buckets in the house, depending on the property size, to be used in case of an emergency. A human chain from canal to fire was built. As of 1610, building houses with wooden facades was forbidden and later it was also forbidden to renovate them at all.

During later centuries the importance of transportation by water declined and the wharves fell into decay. In the last century the city decided to restore them. All of them were private property, but most parties voluntarily donated their lot to the city. The rest were forced to do so. The biggest problem was the sewer system. Normally these are put underneath the streets in front of the houses, but on the side of the canals, the roofs of the wharf cellars lay there and there was no space. Other parts were private property and the wharves were filled with trees. Eventually, in the 1980s, the sewers were dug underneath the water level. The last house by the canal didn't have a closed sewer system until 2007.

The water is now clear of human waste, except for the occasional drunk 'powdering his nose' from the top of a bridge. Most cellars are in use as restaurants and galleries, some are apartments. The wharves are one big terrace and the best place to sit in the sunshine city. The water fills up with bicycle boats, canoes, tour boats and yachts. If you get lucky you might see the 'beer boat' passing; a boat that stocks the restaurants with drinks and food. Also the garbage is transported out by boat.

The canals are alive again and the wharves a unique souvenir of Middle Aged wit.

~~~

7. Practical Information

7.1 Eating

There is not too much to be said about the Dutch eating culture. We are not internationally known for our cuisine. We just gave way to talented chefs from other countries, which is why you can find a restaurant from almost any country in the world in Utrecht. Or you can try your luck at one of the snack bars for a more typical Dutch experience. 'Haute hamburgers' are a trend, but these places are usually filled to the brim. If you would like to read a little bit more about Dutch breakfast culture and our love for mayonnaise, you can read the book 'Peace and Porridge'.

There are many good places in town and only one tourist traps (so far). Restaurants come in all price ranges. If you want to know more about Utrecht and food, buy 'Utrecht & food' on Amazon. https://amzn.to/35zDiV5

Wharves
You should eat in one of the wharf cellars at least

once, because there is nothing else like it and the atmosphere is unparalleled. You can try all flavors, from Thai, Indian and Argentinian to pancakes, the latter being the most typical Dutch. In summer you can sit outside next to the water amongst what seems to be the entire population of Utrecht and beyond. You can find most restaurants between *Lange Smeestraat* and *Lange Viestraat*. Most of them have a sign on the road above and some even a menu, so just walk by and take your pick. On warm days there will be hardly any seats left outside, so you should make a reservation.

Pancakes
Pannenkoekenbakkerij De Muntkelder
Go safe with bacon and cheese, or go wild with sunflower seeds or warm peanut sauce.
Address: Oudegracht 112
Open: Mon – Sun 12:00 -21:00.
Web: http://www.deoudemuntkelder.nl/en/

Argentinian
Gauchos Grill Restaurant
Great steaks.
Address: Oudegracht 150
Open: Mon – Sun 17:00 – 23:00.
Web: https://www.gauchosgrill.nl/restaurants/oude-gracht/
(only Dutch)

Music restaurant
't Oude Pothuys
Menus come on old records and there is daily live music later in the evening.

Address: Oudegracht 279
Open: Every day. Times not revealed.
Web: http://www.pothuys.nl/contact/ (only Dutch)

Town

Alongside the street level of the Old Canal are many
more restaurants. Same goes for *Neude* Square and
the following streets: *Zakkendragerssteeg,
Drieharingstraat, Ganzenmarkt, Schoutenstraat,
Voorstraat, Biltstraat, Nachtegaalstraat,
Servetstraat*. All over downtown, finding a place to
eat shouldn't be difficult. Of course there is also food
in the shopping mall *Hoog Catharijne*, but I cannot
think of any reason to spend your dinner time there.

Grand Restaurant Karel V
Mentioned in the Michelin Guide.
Address: Geertebolwerk 1
Open: Mon – Sat 18:00 – 22:00.
Web: http://www.karelv.nl/en/home/

Bistronome des Arts
Pricy, but with a sun porch above the canal.
Address: Lijnmarkt 48
Open: Wed – Sun 17:30 – 24:00.
Web: http://restaurantlebistronome.com/ (Dutch and French)

Le Jardin ('The Garden')
Vegetables are most important here. There is a
greenhouse in the middle of the restaurant. They sell
flowers as well. Reservations might be required.
Address: Mariaplaats 42

Open: Tue – Sat 12:00 – 15:00 and 17:00 – 24:00.
Web: http://www.lejardinutrecht.nl/ (only Dutch)

Luden
Terrace in a courtyard. Tranquility in the middle of the city.
Address: Janskerkhof 10
Open: Mon – Sat open at 12:00.
Web: http://www.ludenutrecht.nl/ (only Dutch)

Budget options:

Kartoffel ('Potato')
German style.
Address: Oudegracht aan de Werf 145
Web: http://kartoffelutrecht.nl/ (only Dutch, menu partly German)

Eazie
Asian fast food.
Address: Voorstraat 8
Open: Mon – Sun 12:00 – 22:00.
Web: http://eazie.nl/en/restaurants/

Supermarket
Boon's markt
Address: Ganzenmarkt 2-6
Open: Mon – Sat 08:00 – 24:00, Sun 10:00 – 24:00.
Web: http://www.boonsmarkt.nl/ (only Dutch)

View, cookies and breakfast
Let us look at the upside: 85% of Utrechters fulfill the breakfast norm. I have no idea what that means,

but follow our example and eat well. There are possibilities for breakfast in several places, the cheapest in town probably being the one in department store *Hema*. A cosy option is The Discovery (*De Ontdekking*) and a more budget option is the Eastern German inspired *Puschkin*, in a former garage. (There is a video on our channel.) Holes in sweet teeth can be filled by a bakery in Saddle Street (*Zadelstraat*). They sell Miffy cookies and 'Dom Towers' (*Domtorentjes*); chocolate filled with chocolate. They also have the 'French cruller' that our town is known for, called *sprits* in singular, but who would eat only one? In this same street, in front of number 11, is a special tile. It shows you where the Dom Tower would lie if it fell over this way. Hypothetically speaking.

And if you literally love the upside, you can eat at a restaurant in a former water tower, from which you have a nice view over the city from the south side.

Department store *Hema*
There are several in town, this is the most central one. € 2,00.
Address: Steenweg 59 & Oudegracht
Open: At 09:00, breakfast served until 10:00. Not available on Sundays.
Web: http://www.hema.nl/nieuws/ontbijt (only Dutch)

De Ontdekking ('The Discovery')
Address: Voorstraat 110
Open: Mon – Fri 08:00 – 19:00, Sat & Sun 09:00 – 19:00.

Web: http://www.deontdekkingutrecht.nl/ (only Dutch)

Puschkin
Address: Ridderschapstraat 1
Open: Mon – Fri 08:00 – 18:00, Sat & Sun 09:00 – 18:00.
Web: https://www.facebook.com/Puschkin-OntbijtLunch-474107356129949/info?tab=page_info

Bakery
Bakkerij Theo Blom
Address: Zadelstraat 23
Open: Mon & Sat 08:00 – 17:00, Tue – Fri 08:00 – 18:00.
Web: http://www.banketbakkerijtheoblom.nl/view.asp?page=producten (only Dutch)

Water Tower Utrecht
WT Urban Kitchen
Address: Heuveloord 25A
Open: Mon – Thu 17:30 – 24:00, Fri – Sun 12:00 – 24:00.
Web: https://wturbankitchen.nl/ (only Dutch)

7.2 Anthem

There is an unofficial city song, written and sang by *Herman Bertien*. A small statue of the singer stands in town, on a square called *Ledig Erf*.

Als ik boven op de Dom sta
kijk ik even naar benee
dan zie ik het oude gragie
het Vreeburg en Wijk C
Ja, dan springt m'n hartsie open
ik ben trots wat dag ie wat
der is geen mooier plehekie
als Utereg M'n stad
als Utereg M'n stad

Utereg m'n stadsie daar gebeurt van alle hand
het bruist aan alle kant in het hartsie van het land
de sterrenwijk het houtplein en de Lange
Rozendaal
Utereg het mooist van allemaal

"When I stand on top of the Dom Tower
I look down
and see the Old Canal
the Peace Fortress Square and Neighbourhood C
and then my heart jumps
I am proud, what would you think?
There is no nicer place

than Utrecht my town.

Utrecht my city, lots of things happen there
it bursts on all sides in this heart of the country
the Star Neighbourhood and the Long Roses Street
Utrecht is the prettiest of all."

Check out the music on Youtube here:
https://www.youtube.com/watch?v=XEJMseCgkz8

7.3 Safety

Hardship hits all times and places. Utrecht has had its share. The hurricane that hit the city in 1674 ruined a lot of buildings, including the ship of the Dom Church. Spanish, French and German occupations diminished the people's spirits and city funds, as well as the plaque and the cholera, economic downfall and declining beer production. Crime is of all times too, and the stealing of bikes is the most common one. Make sure you attach your bicycle properly with several locks and don't just lock your front wheel to a balustrade. You wouldn't be the first who is left with nothing but a lock and one tire.

You are safe wandering around town, but don't forget that you probably stick out like a tourist and thieves love those. So be smart with your smart phone, wallet and everything you don't want others to sell for you on eBay. Most pickpocketing takes place in the city center. As tourism rises, so will this.

Most outer areas are safe, but use common sense and avoid walking alone through dark parks or alleys, as you would anywhere. The neighborhood called *Overvecht* has a higher crime rate and no sights, except for the slide at its train station. Passengers can slide straight from the street to the platform. *The Rough Guide* has mentioned it in its list of 11 best slides in the world.

Most hazardous is the traffic downtown. The streets are used by bicycles and cars, but most others think that the entire city center is a pedestrian zone. Also keep your eyes out for mopeds of food deliverers. They know no mercy.

You might see a homeless person selling a newspaper or singing you a song. Feel free to sing along. There are some beggars showing up in the streets. This is allowed in Utrecht. Some may be homeless people from the city, or illegal aliens. There is also talk of gangs sent out to beg. So far they don't pose any problems.

The homeless newspaper, Street News (*Straatnieuws*), had five minutes of world fame in 2015. Pope Francis had never been interviewed by a Dutch journalist before, but the homeless *Marc* managed to get an interview. He discovered that the pope had wanted to be a butcher when he was a kid. *Marc* is not a Catholic, but called the pope a 'great guy' and said this meeting had made him a new person. *Marc* is the most famous newspaper seller in town. His article won the 'Special News Service Award'.

7.4 King's Day

King's Day originated in Utrecht. On August 31st 1885 the first 'Princess Day' was organized on the fifth birthday of Princess Wilhelmina in Neighborhood C. After her father, King Willem III, died, it turned into Queen's Day and spread to other cities. After the Second World War, the celebrations became nationwide.

For many years, this day was celebrated on April 30th, since Queen Juliana (reign 1948-1980) had her birthday on that day. The birthday of her daughter Beatrix (reign 1980-2013) was in January. A lot of the celebrations take place outside, so she decided to maintain the holiday on the 30th. This was also the day on which she became queen. In 2013 we got a king, Willem-Alexander, who has his birthday on April 27th. Ever since, this day has been on the national list of intangible cultural heritage. Many tourists with old guide books still come to the country on April 30th, to find only the remnants of the celebrations.

The night before is the so called 'King's Night'. There are markets everywhere, so called 'free markets', because there are no licenses required. Anyone can sit down and sell whatever garbage or talent they offer. A lot of people are in some way dressed in orange or wear orange accessories. There are also many parties and live music. On the last

Friday before King's Day the schools have their 'King's Games'. They have breakfast together and then a day filled with sports and games.

The royal family visits one or two towns where they play traditional, and sometimes less traditional, games and watch bands, choirs, traditional dancing and trades. The city wants the King to celebrate the day in Utrecht in one of the coming years. After all, King Willem-Alexander was born in Utrecht. This was the year 1967, in the Academic Hospital, which was then situated in *Nicolaas Beetsstraat*.

7.5 Sleeping

It is not a cheap city to stay in. Even a hostel room can set you back € 61. The cheapest bed is € 22.40, no sheets included (2020).

Upscale:

Charles V
Karel V
Address: Geertebolwerk 1
Web: http://www.karelv.nl/en/home/

Design:

Mother Goose
Address: Ganzenmarkt 26
Web: http://www.mothergoosehotel.com/en

Eye Hotel
Nominated for the Hospitality & Style Award 2015.
Address: Wijde Begijnestraat 1-3
Web: http://www.eyehotel.nl/en

Hotel Simple
Address: Domstraat 4
Web: http://simpleutrecht.nl/Hotel/

Mary K Hotel
Address: Oudegracht 25
Web: https://www.marykhotel.com/?lang=en

Hotel Badhu

Every room is different, each with its own color and everything in the room is adjusted to that. They also have a restaurant and bar.
Address: Willem van Noortplein 19
Web: http://www.badhu.nl/hotel (only Dutch)

Budget:

Stone Hotel & Hostel
Address: Biltstraat 31
Web: http://www.stonehotel.nl/en/

Stayoke Hostel
They have dorms and private rooms. For families they have a special Miffy room and a railwaymuseum room.
Address: Neude 4-5
Web: https://www.stayokay.com/en/hostel/utrecht-centrum (English)
https://www.stayokay.com/de/hostel/utrecht-centrum (Deutsch)

Hostel Strowis
Address: Boothstraat 8
Web: http://www.strowis.nl/

Klein Armelisweerd
Cheapest option for couples having no demands at all. They have huts at the edge of town without electricity or water. They also have spaces for campers. It is partially run by the people living there, who have psychiatric problems.
Address: Koningsweg 358
Web: http://www.kleinarmelisweerd.nl/gastenverblijven (only Dutch)

Budget Camping Utrecht
Address: Ariënslaan 5
Web: https://www.budgetcampingutrecht.nl/index_en.html
(English)

More hotels can be booked on:
http://www.hotels.nl/nl/utrecht/

Airbnb offers options in all price ranges. Advantage can be to have more contact with the locals and get more insider information. Or stay at my place: http://bit.ly/1U7DQHH.

7.6 Sinterklaas

Sinterklaas is a very old bishop. Nobody knows his real age, but his white beard is very long. So is his hair. He lives in Spain and always comes to Holland with a steamboat loaded with presents. Of course he cannot do all the work himself, so he has a lot of helpers, called Black Pete (*Zwarte Piet*). They are always silly and foolish and they have a terrible taste for fashion, but they spread the candy! There is special Sinterklaas candy called *pepernoten* and some other sweets (marzipan for example) shaped for the occasion. And everybody gets the first letter of his name in chocolate. You can find these in stores as of September.

The Saint has a thick book in which he can read which children have been good and which ones haven't. The bad ones shall be put into a bag and taken to Spain! But this doesn't happen a lot these days. Grownups are begging to be taken on the ship, but they are not the ones this special day is about. At the end of November the boat arrives in Holland and the huge crew starts with the preparations. If the kids put out their shoe at night, a bowl of water or a carrot for the horse and sing a special Saint song, they may find a small present or some candy in their shoe the next day. They have to put their shoe next to the chimney, because the Saint rides his grey horse over the roof tops and the Black Petes bring the presents in through the chimney. For some mysterious reason children living in a house with central heating get presents too.

When the day of the real celebration comes, kids get several presents. And as long as the children are young and thought to still 'believe', the adults wrap up something for themselves as well. Some adult groups celebrate the party by 'picking a lot' (*lootje trekken*). Everybody writes his name on a small piece of paper and possibly some gift ideas. Afterwards everybody picks a lot and buys a present for that person. Depending on the amount of creativity and time at hand, these gifts come with a mock poem and wrapped in a home fabricated object. For example, if somebody talks too much, you could craft a 1 meter wide mouth to wrap up the earrings she wanted, accompanied with a poem saying:
"Sinterklaas was thinking
what he would give to you
something for your ears
but maybe you can use it for your mouth too."

More on the subject:
http://www.intochtutrecht.nl/ (only Dutch)
http://bit.ly/1OgojDk (English)
the songs: https://www.youtube.com/watch?v=vG5Xr8uQ5l8

7.7 Transportation

Utrecht can be reached by train, car, bicycle, boat and plane. There are no border controls on land with the neighboring countries.
Travel times by train from:

Amsterdam	00:27 -	53 km (33 miles)
Brussels	02:17 -	180 km (112 miles)
Paris	03:36 -	480 km (298 miles)
London	04:55 -	500 km (311 miles)
Berlin	06:02 -	633 km (393 miles)

By plane, Amsterdam is connected with the entire world. There is a train station underneath the airport, taking you to Utrecht in 33 minutes.

Eindhoven Airport has a frequent bus connection to the city center. From there you can go onwards by train (50 minutes). There are cheap flights from many destinations in Europe and northern Africa. Try RyanAir or WizzAir for budget prices. Rotterdam Airport has similar flights, but fewer connections.

Tickets for the train cannot be bought on board. There are vending machines at the train station. Buy your ticket before you go to the platforms. Some buses do sell tickets, but they are very expensive.

Most Dutch people have a 'public transportation card' (*OV-kaart*) that they scan when they travel and they pay through this card. As a tourist you could buy a so-called 'anonymous card', available at train stations, tobacco stores and supermarkets. The card costs € 7.50 (2020). This is just for the card. After that, you have to go to a special card machine to load money on it. There are several ways to pay, a credit card not being one of them. With this debit you can travel, if the amount of money that is left on the card is enough for the beginning fare of the trip. There will always be some money left on it and you can have restored to you. For this service you have to pay € 1 and manage to find an open and manned counter of one of the participating transporters. An alternative is an expensive one-way ticket.

By now you probably prefer the idea walking. The easiest way to get to Utrecht is by train and the city center is so small that there is no need for the hassle. Just put on your walking shoes. Or your blue suede ones. If you don't have any, you can buy them at the Elvis Corner.

Taxis will have a hard time riding around downtown, as any car does. You could, however, use one from the outskirts to the city center, or vice versa. It won't always be easy to get one on the street, so ask somebody to call one for you. You pay around € 2.10 per kilometer and € 0.30 per minute, plus a start fee. Around the city, a taxi will hardly ever cost more than € 14.00.

If you come to Utrecht by car, park it on the outskirts and enter the town using public

transportation:
https://www.parkeren-utrecht.nl/pr

7.8 Tours

Gilde Utrecht ('Guild of Utrecht')
Tours on specific themes. Most guides speak several
languages.
https://www.gildeutrecht.nl/english
https://www.gildeutrecht.nl/deutsch
https://www.gildeutrecht.nl/francais

Free Tours
Always in English.
Video of our tour: http://bit.ly/1YboG77.
When: Tue, Wed, Sat & Sun 12:00, themed tours on Sat 10:00
and Sun 14:00
Where: Just show up underneath the Dom Tower and follow the
person in the red shirt.
Web: http://www.utrechtfreetours.nl/

Tourist Information Center
VVV
Several options with either a group or route maps.
Address: Domplein 9
Web: http://www.visit-utrecht.com/explore-utrecht/city-tours
(English)
http://www.besuch-utrecht.de/utrecht-
entdecken/stadtfuhrung (Deutsch)

Color Bike Tours
Two options: City Tour and Multiculti Tour.
Address: Mariaplaats 2.
Web: http://www.biketourutrecht.com/

Holland is the largest exporter of bikes in Europe and also the largest producer. In 2015 the export worth of bicycles was 793 million euros.

Utrecht Underground Tour

An (ex) addict and/or homeless person leads you through the other side of town. Only to be paid by invoice and after reservation.
Web: http://www.utrechtunderground.nl/

Light Tour

Trajectum Lumen
There is a tour through town leading you past 'light art' near or at different buildings in town. There is a path of circular lamps in the pavement you can follow. Some sights are simply lit buildings. Some light art only shows once every hour, which is not very practical if you are walking around town when it is dark and therefore maybe cold, depending on your luck with the weather.
There is also a free app describing the art works. There are guided tours every Saturday evening. You have to make a reservation in advance.
Web: http://www.trajectumlumen.com/en/
App: http://www.trajectumlumen.com/en/map

Food & Drinks Tour

Let your taste buds lead you through Utrecht. The guide will lead you through the day, from breakfast to late night drinks, and also includes a suggested 1-day itinerary with map: http://amzn.to/1XijfEg.

Schuttevaer

One hour boat tour through the canal and moat.
Where: Opposite Oudegracht 85
Web: http://www.schuttevaer.com/nl/boat-excursions-and-
tours-over-unique-canal-system-mediaeval-city-utrecht
(English)
http://www.schuttevaer.com/nl/bootfahrt-oder-rundfahrt-
%C3%BCber-die-einmaligen-grachten-der-mittelalterlichen-
stadt-utrecht (Deutsch)

Compass App

Roaming around yourself might be easier with the app
'Dompas'. It is a compass that doesn't show north, but
towards the Dom Tower. Always.
http://dompas.nl

7.9 Wilhelm-Ray

Did you know that Wilhelm Röntgen, inventor of the famous X-rays, lived in Utrecht? He was born of a German father and a Dutch mother. He attended grammar school in the city of Apeldoorn in the east of Holland. After that he went to the trade school in Utrecht. One day another student drew a cartoon of his teacher. Wilhelm got the blame for this, but didn't want to snitch on his friend and so he was expelled from school. Therefore, he was not allowed to study physics at the Utrecht University and he moved to Switzerland. In the *Schalkwijkstraat,* you can see a tiled picture on the house he lived in during his time in Utrecht.

7. 10 Language

English		Dutch
hello	-	hallo
hi	-	hoi
buy	-	doei
goodbye	-	tot ziens
yes	-	ja
no	-	nee
maybe	-	misschien
sorry	-	sorry
please	-	alsjeblieft
thank you	-	bedankt / dank je
good	-	goed
bad	-	slecht
great!	-	geweldig
How much is?	-	Hoeveel kost...?
Help!	-	Help!
good morning	-	goedemorgen
good afternoon	-	goedemiddag
good evening	-	goedenavond
My name is...	-	Ik heet ....
I am from ...	-	Ik kom uit ....
Germany	-	Duitsland
United Kingdom	-	Engeland
France	-	Frankrijk
Spain	-	Spanje
Italy	-	Italië
USA	-	Amerika

Ireland	-	Ierland
Poland	-	Polen
Morocco	-	Marokko
Turkey	-	Turkije
Switzerland	-	Zwitserland
Panama	-	Panama
shelf company	-	brievenbusfirma
Do you speak..	-	Spreekt u .. (formal)
		Spreek je .. (informal)
English	-	Engels
German	-	Duits
French	-	Frans
Spanish	-	Spaans
Arabic	-	Arabisch
Polish	-	Pools
Italian	-	Italiaans
Monday	-	maandag
Tuesday	-	dinsdag
Wednesday	-	woensdag
Thursday	-	donderdag
Friday	-	vrijdag
Saturday	-	zaterdag
Sunday	-	zondag
nit picker	-	mierenneuker
January	-	januari
February	-	februari
March	-	maart
April	-	april
May	-	mei
June	-	juni

July	-	juli
August	-	augustus
September	-	september
October	-	oktober
November	-	november
December	-	december
closed	-	gesloten
open	-	open
opening hours	-	openingstijden
holiday	-	vakantie
doctor	-	dokter
hospital	-	ziekenhuis
ill	-	ziek
I swallowed a frog.	-	Ik heb een kikker ingeslikt.
Police	-	politie
fire brigade	-	brandweer
hotel	-	hotel
room	-	kamer
bathroom	-	badkamer
key	-	sleutel
single room	-	eenpersoonskamer
double room	-	tweepersoonskamer
breakfast	-	ontbijt
lunch	-	lunch
dinner	-	avondeten / diner
WiFi	-	Wifi
camping	-	camping
bed	-	bed

pillow	-	kussen
shed	-	schuur
museum	-	museum
church	-	kerk
tower	-	toren
ticket	-	kaartje
ATM	-	pinautomaat
restaurant	-	restaurant
coffee	-	koffie
tea	-	thee
milk	-	melk
sugar	-	suiker
beer	-	bier
wine	-	wijn
chocolate sprinkles	-	hagelslag
ice cream	-	ijs
French Fries	-	patat / friet
too expensive	-	te duur
too cheap	-	te goedkoop
bicycle	-	fiets
car	-	auto
bus	-	bus
train	-	trein
plane	-	vliegtuig
parking lot	-	parkeergarage
flat tire	-	lekke band
for rent	-	te huur
for sale	-	te koop

| sales | - | uitverkoop |

| I love Utrecht. | - | Ik hou van Utrecht. |
| What time is it? | - | Hoe laat is het? |

1	-	een
2	-	twee
3	-	drie
4	-	vier
5	-	vijf
6	-	zes
7	-	zeven
8	-	acht
9	-	negen
10	-	tien
11	-	elf
12	-	twaalf
13	-	dertien
14	-	veertien
15	-	vijftien
16	-	zestien
17	-	zeventien
18	-	achttien
19	-	negentien
20	-	twintig
30	-	dertig
40	-	veertig
50	-	vijftig

60	-	zestig
70	-	zeventig
80	-	tachtig
90	-	negentig
100	-	honderd
1,000	-	duizend
1,000,000	-	1 miljoen

7.11 Peace

Beyond Dutch borders, Utrecht is most known for its peace treaty. There had been a war going on, mainly between France and Spain, since 1701. The first of a series of treaties to end this was signed on April 11th in Utrecht. The negotiations took place in the city hall. Many delegates came to town and stayed for 1.5 years, giving a huge economic boost to the city, although some left without paying. One more time Utrecht seemed to be the center of the European universe, but it was only as a host. As the French negotiator Melchior de Polignac put it: "About you, around you, without you."

7.12 Special Days

National Holidays are marked with NH.

✳ New Year's Day **NH**
January 1st

✳ Valentine's Day
February 14th
Not a traditional Dutch celebration, but shops sell hearts and lots of pink stuff.

✳ Carnival
February 23rd - 25th (2020), February 14th - 16th (2021)
In some towns around Utrecht there are big parades. The one in Utrecht is comparatively small. You might run into some people dressed as idiots, clowns or both.

✳ 1st Easter Day (always a Sunday) **NH**
✳ 2nd Easter Day (always a Monday) **NH**
April 12th and 13th (2020), April 4th and 5th (2021)

✳ King's Day **NH**
April 27th
Except if this is a Sunday, then it will be celebrated on April 26th.

✳ Ascension Day (always a Thursday) **NH**
May 21st (2020), May 13th (2021)

✳ Memorial Day
May 4th
A normal working day. At 20:00 there is a nationwide 2 minute silence in remembrance of the WWII victims and there are flowers laid at different memorial sites.

✳ Liberation Day
May 5th
Most public services are closed on this day. Others have a day off only every five years (the next in 2020), but it is different in every branch. There are a lot of music festivals.

✳ 1st Pentecost Day (always a Sunday) **NH**
✳ 2nd Pentecost Day (always a Monday) **NH**
May 31st and June 1st (2020), May 23rd and 24th (2021)

✳ Prince's Day / Budget Day
The third Tuesday in September.
This day the King rides around The Hague in a carriage and the government unveils its plans for the next year. Other than that, life functions as normal.

✳ Halloween
October 31st
Not a traditional Dutch celebration, but shops sell some Halloween related items and there might be a party or two.

✳ Saint Martin
November 11th
Big festival in Utrecht with lots of activities, especially the Saturday and Sunday before November 11th.

✷ Sinterklaas
December 5th
This is a special fest, because it is only celebrated in The Netherlands (and some of the Caribbean Islands that were once part of our kingdom) and in some parts of Germany and Belgium. Three weeks before, Sinterklaas arrives in town by boat. The arrival of the real Sinterklaas is broadcasted on national television (November 16th 2019, November 14th 2020). This is in a different city every year. Fake ones (don't tell the kids!) arrive in every town.

✷ 1st Christmas Day **NH**
December 25th
✷ 2nd Christmas Day **NH**
December 26th

School Vacations
There are several school vacations throughout the year. The country is divided into 3 regions which have different dates off, to spread the crowds. If you want to avoid the masses, check out when each vacation is:
2020: https://www.schoolvakanties-nederland.nl/schoolvakanties-2020.html
2021: https://www.schoolvakanties-nederland.nl/schoolvakanties-2021.html
Basisonderwijs = elementary school
Voortgezet onderwijs = high school
Utrecht is in the middle region: *midden*.

148

7. 13 Events, festivals and the like

This is just a selection, there is too much going on to be listed in this book. A lot of dates were not yet know at the time of writing.

Sports
Calendar for Sports Events: http://www.sportstad-utrecht.nl/agenda/ (only Dutch)
There are many possibilities for cycle racing, running and skating.

Utrecht Science Park Marathon
When: April 19th 2020
Web: http://www.utrechtmarathon.com/ (only Dutch)

Singelloop
Run 10 km (6.2 miles) through the city center of Utrecht.
When: October 4th (2020)
Web: http://www.singellooputrecht.nl/ (only Dutch)

Music:

Free Classical Concerts
Free lunch break concerts by students from the music academy. When played, it is on a Monday 12:30 – 13:00. Never in vacation time and it is an irregular schedule. There is a clear schedule on the web.
Address: Korte Minrebroederstraat 2 (Old City Hall)
Web: https://www.utrecht.nl/wonen-en-leven/vrije-tijd/stadhuis/culturele-activiteiten/lunchconcert-studenten-conservatorium-hku/ (only Dutch)

Free concerts are also given in the concert hall *TivoliVredenburg* by Young Talent. They start at 12:30. The room is called *Hertz* and if you are late you won't be let in. It is on most Fridays, but not all. For this, you would have to check the schedule or email/call. The schedule should say *lunchpauzeconcert*.
Address: Vredenburgkade 11
Web: https://www.tivolivredenburg.nl/nl/ (only Dutch)

In July and August there are free classical concerts in the courtyard that leads towards the Museum of Christianity. It is open air.
When: July and August at 13:30 and 15:00.
Where: Lange Nieuwstraat 38
Web: https://www.catharijneconvent.nl/activiteiten/ (only Dutch)

Record & CD fair
The biggest twice a year in the Year Fair, around November and April.
There are smaller ones almost every week:
http://www.platenbeurzen.com/ (only Dutch)

Festival Early music
Festival Oude Muziek
When: Aug 28th – Sept 6th 2020
(Aug 27th – Sept 5th 2021)
Web: http://oudemuziek.nl/home/

Le Guess Who?
Avant-garde music.
When: November 12th - 15th 2020
Web: http://leguesswho.nl/

Jazz Festival (1 stage)
Utrechts Jazz Festival
When: July 2019, date 2020 unknown
Where: Janskerkhof
Web: http://www.utrechtsjazzfestival.nl/ (only Dutch)

Lazy Sunday Afternoon
Free music in the park. Bring your own picnic.
Where: Park Lepelenburg, Nieuwegracht Oost
When: 13:00 – 17:00 during several summer Sundays.
Schedule:
http://www.zimihc.nl/spotlights/zimihcmaatwerk/werk/lazy-sunday-afternoon/ (only Dutch)

Klein New Orleans
Gumbo, brass and rock 'n roll in the middle of the street.
Where: Breestraat
When: May 31st 2020
Web: http://www.kleinneworleans.nl/

Food:

Food Truck Festival
TREK
Watch a short video about this event: http://bit.ly/22UkLw9.
Where: Griftpark
When: June 2020
Web: https://www.festival-trek.nl/trek-utrecht/ (only Dutch)

Spoon Spoon
Lepeltje Lepeltje
Mobile kitchens, music and vintage.
Where: Lepelenburg

When: June 2020
Web: http://www.lepeltje-lepeltje.com/utrecht/ (only Dutch)

Beer Brewery Festival
PINT Utrechtse Bierbrouwers Festival
When: May 2020
Web: http://www.houtensbrouwcollectief.nl/ (only Dutch)

Culture:

Holland Animation Film Festival
Where: Different locations.
When: Maybe November 2020, unclear due to a reorganization
Web: https://www.facebook.com/HAFFnl (only Dutch)

Spring Festival
International dance and theater.
Where: Several locations downtown.
When: May 14th - 23rd (2020)
Web: https://www.springutrecht.nl/?language=en

Dutch Film Festival
When: September 25th – Oct 3rd 2020
Web: https://www.filmfestival.nl/en/

Beginning of cultural season
Uitfeest
The first Cultural Sunday in September (September 12th and 13th 2020) there are a lot of performances around town from all kinds of different arts. It is traditionally the weekend where the theaters etc. show what is on offer in the cultural year to come.

Open Garden Day
Open tuinen dag
Private gardens downtown open their gates for a day. You have to buy a day pass. Tickets are for sale at the tourist information center and on the day itself also at Grand Hotel Karel V and the Museum of Christianity.
When: June 27th (2020)
Web: http://opentuinendagutrecht.nl/informatie/ (only Dutch)

Open Monuments Day
Open Monumentendag
Many monuments are open for free, some are open only this weekend.
When: September 12th and 13th 2020
Web: http://www.openmonumentendag.nl/open-monumentendag-english-summary/

International Literature Festival
All about the art of writing and (international) famous writers. Promises to be bigger every year, now that Utrecht has been named City of Literature by UNESCO since 2017.
When: Second half of September (2020)
Web: http://www.ilfu.nl/en

Midsummer Canal Festival
Midzomer Gracht Festival
Utrecht celebrating sexual & gender diversity. Parties, music, lectures, expositions. As of 2017 there is a yearly Gay Pride Parade.
When: June 19th - 27th (2020)
Web: http://www.midzomergracht.nl/

Rainbow zebra: On the crossing of *Lange Viestraat* and *Saint Jacobsstraat*, underneath the Miffy traffic light, is a rainbow zebra crossing.

LGBTH traffic light: On the junction of *Daalsestraat* and *Knipstraat*, a little further to the north east, are three traffic lights: one with a gay couple, one with a lesbian couple and one with a heterosexual couple.

154

7.14 Cold Shelter

Underneath the train station is a tunnel called Northern Tunnel (*Noordertunnel*). It is now a way to walk to either the west or the east part of the city, but during the cold war it was a bomb shelter. There are white letters on the floor stating: "During the '60s and '70s this passage way could be used as a bomb shelter and accommodate 2,000 people for 48 hours." Red stripes show the size.

There used to be a piece of wall replaced by glass, through which you can see steel doors and a few showers. In another area that was not visible for the public, was a storage room with assembly kits for bunk beds, drinking water and emergency rations. It was the only bomb shelter underneath a train station left in The Netherlands.

Because of the ongoing construction in this area, this too has become history. The contents of the shelter shall be relocated to a museum.

7.15 Going Out

Cinemas in the center
(Most movies are broadcasted in the original language and subtitled in Dutch.)

Art House:

Louis Hartlooper Complex
Address: Tolsteegbrug 1
Web: http://www.hartlooper.nl/en (only Dutch)

Springhaver
Address: Springweg 46
Web: http://www.springhaver.nl/ (only Dutch)

Mainstream:

Kinepolis
Address: Jaarbeursplein
Web: https://kinepolis.nl/bioscopen/kinepolis-jaarbeurs?main-section=presales# (only Dutch)

Pathé Rembrandt
Address: Oudegracht 73
Web: https://www.pathe.nl/bioscoop/rembrandt (only Dutch)

Theatres:

Stadschouwburg
Address: Lucasbolwerk 24

https://stadsschouwburg-utrecht.nl/english/buy-tickets/

Schiller Theatre
Intimate, enlarged living room.
Address: Minrebroederstraat 11
Web: http://www.schillertheater.nl/ (only Dutch)

Beatrix Theatre (grand musicals)
Address: Jaarbeursplein 6A
Web: http://www.stage-entertainment.nl/theaters/beatrix-theater-utrecht/

Werftheater (in a wharf cellar)
Address: Oudegracht 60
Web: http://www.werftheater.nl/ (only Dutch)

Theater Kikker ('Frog Theatre')
Not mainstream.
Address: Ganzenmarkt 14
Web: https://www.theaterkikker.nl/category/engels-voor-lnp/

Discos:

Basis
Address: Oudegracht aan de Werf 97
Web: http://www.clubbasis.nl/ (only Dutch)

Club Poema
Address: Drieharingstraat 22
Web: http://clubpoema.nl/ (only Dutch)

De Nachtburgemeester
Address: Stadhuisbrug 3

Wooloomooloo
Student disco.
Open: Mon, Wed – Sat 23:00 – 05:00
Address: Janskerkhof 14
Web: https://www.zaalverhuur-utrecht.nl/evenementen/ (only Dutch)

Music:

Ekko (popular)
Address: Bemuurde Weerd WZ 3
Web: http://ekko.nl/ (only Dutch)

TivoliVredenburg (popular and classic)
Address: Vredenburgkade 11
Web: https://www.tivolivredenburg.nl/nl/ (only Dutch)

Bars and Cafes:

The city is stuffed with them. A small random selection:

Stairway to Heaven
Owned by a Dutch musician. The building used to be a stable providing the horses for the trams. Serves high tea and high beer (reservation necessary).
Address: Mariaplaats 11
Web: http://www.stairway.nl/ (only Dutch)

Cafe DeRat
In 1978 the new owner discovered a petrified rat in the cellar, hence the name 'TheRat' (*de rat*). Old town cafe atmosphere. Large collection of beer and whiskey.

Address: Lange Smeestraat 37
Web: http://www.cafederat.nl/ (only Dutch)

Cafe Hofman

Once a month during school season there is
'philosophical cafe'. All kinds of other activities. Check
the schedule.
Address: Janskerkhof 17a
Web: http://hofman-cafe.nl/en/

Mick O'Connells - Irish Pub

Address: Jansdam 3

Cafe Orloff

An oldy. Small but good atmosphere. Breakfast, lunch,
dinner, drinks.
Address: Donkere Gaard 6-8
Web: http://orloff.nl/ (only Dutch)
Now has a modern, less authentic sister on a future
hotspot:

Orloff aan de Kade

Address: Oosterkade 18
Web: http://orloffaandekade.nl/ (only Dutch)

Oude Dikke Dries ('old fat Dries')

Folksy cafe.
Address: Waterstraat 32.
Web: http://ouwedikkedries.nl/ (only Dutch)

Cafe Marktzicht

This is one of the oldest cafes in Utrecht. It has been here
since 1898. Local pub atmosphere, young staff.
Address: Breedstraat 4
Open: Mon – Fri 10:30 – 02:30, Sat 07:00 – 02:30, Sun 12:00
– 24:00.

Web: http://marktzicht.intercafe.nl/over/ (only Dutch and probably as old as the cafe itself)

't Gras van de Buren ('the neighbour's grass')
Address: Lange Jansstraat 16
Web: http://grasvandeburen.nl/

ACU
Political Cultural Center with concerts, vegan & vegetarian food, cafe, events, lectures, movies. Run by volunteers. According to some it is a left wing center with lots of dreadlocks, but it depends on the activity and everybody is welcome.
Address: Voorstraat 71
Open: Tue, Wed 18:00 – 23:00, Thu 18:00 – 03:00, Fri 20:00 – 04:00, Sat 18:00 – 04:00, Sun 14:00 – 2:00
Web: http://acu.nl/ (mainly Dutch)

Florin – English Pub
Address: Nobelstraat 2
Web: http://www.florinutrecht.nl/

Body Talk – LGBT
Address: Oudegracht 64
Web: http://www.bodytalk.org/

Cafe Kalff – LGBT
Address: Oudegracht 47
Web: http://www.cafekalff.nl/

PANN – LGBT Parties
Web: http://pann.nl/english/

The Streetfood Club
New place with a spectacular interior.

Address: Janskerkhof 9
Web: https://thestreetfoodclub.nl/

Cafe de Zaak
Always full. Open all day and night and it is allowed to bring your own food.
Address: Korte Minrebroederstraat 9
Web: http://dezaak-utrecht.nl/

De Beurs
For the younger crowd.
Address: Neude 37
Web: https://www.debeursutrecht.nl/en/

Also available:

Utrecht & Food
Let your taste buds lead you through Utrecht.

Utrecht & Children
How to make a city trip with kids even more fun.

Utrecht & Religion
For those fascinated by religion and history.

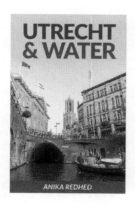

Utrecht & Water
Do you love water and boating? Plunge in.

Thank you for reading!
It would be a great help to us,
if you would leave an online review!

Other books by the same author:
Cappuccino in Jordanië (Dutch only)
Cappuccino in het Midden-Oosten (Dutch only)
Cappuccino in Curaçao (spring 2020)

Inspired by...

De Lantaarn Spreekt. N. Stoppelenburg. Uitgeverij Oud-Utrecht. 2013.

Een paradijs vol weelde. - Geschiedenis van de stad Utrecht. R.E. De Bruin e.a.. 2000

Het stadhuis van Utrecht. J. Jamer e.a.. Het Utrechts archief. 2000

Utrecht, de oude gracht II. Dr A. van Hulzen. Uitgeverij Bekking Amersfoort. 1991

Utrecht en de Cholera 1832 – 1910. P- 't Hart. Uitgeverij Walburg Pers. 1990

Utrecht in steen. - Historische bouwstenen in de binnenstad. W. Dubelaar & T.G. Nijland. Uitgeverij Matrijs. 2012

Several brochures published by the City:
https://erfgoed.utrecht.nl/publicaties/publieksbrochure s-cultuurhistorie-gemeente-utrecht/

Don't miss my new releases and subscribe for special offers!

https://bit.ly/2FRPsyg

Printed in Great Britain
by Amazon